双手好菜

Hunan *A Lifetime of Secrets from Mr Peng's Chinese Kitchen*

Hunan

*A Lifetime of Secrets from
Mr Peng's Chinese Kitchen*

with Qin Xie

Contents

A few words with Mr Peng

Chefs often talk about where they've come from, where they've been, what kitchens they've worked in and who they've worked with. If you asked me what inspired me to start cooking, I honestly don't know. From when I was fourteen years old, I knew that I wanted to work in a kitchen and that was it.

I've always kept my story close to my heart. As far as I'm concerned, all you need to know is that food is my life.

You might think it's strange to have no provenance when food these days is all about having roots but if I show you my hands, you will understand. Wrinkled and bronzed with age, they tell of more than half a century's worth of kitchen stories. The fingers don't quite fully extend because they've become so familiar with the unyielding handles of the cleaver and the wok. Bleached white lines illustrate cuts that are so deep they've become permanently tattooed on the skin. Hardened pads, built up over many years, are as much a necessity as a by-product.

When I opened my restaurant Hunan in 1982, it was a seven-days-a-week operation. Today we are open for six. This is probably the only thing that has changed in the past thirty years.

Life hasn't slowed down at all. Even though I am close to seventy, I'm still in the kitchen and in the restaurant every day doing prep, working the wok and talking to guests, many of whom have been regulars for years.

My statues of Buddha are high up near the ceiling of the restaurant along with some of the antiques I've collected over the years, and my favourite brush paintings line the walls. The hand-written orders are still sent down to the kitchen by a chute and the food still travels up in the dumb waiter. The restaurant has had a lick of paint here and there but fundamentally, it is still the same.

What makes Hunan unique is our approach to dining. I want everyone to try everything, and to try different things every time, so there is no menu. Instead, each guest is served a selection of small dishes, often more than 15 in one sitting. Each plate is a photograph for the palate, capturing memories of Taiwan, Sichuan, Guangdong and beyond.

The food is simple but the flavours are infinite. It is about teasing out the best of the ingredients. Subtle blends of chilli and Sichuan peppercorns push enormous pearly scallops to the edge while keeping them fresh and sweet, and the gentle salty miso cuts through the tenderest slivers of corn-fed chicken to make the most wonderful savoury dish.

With three vinegars, four chilli sauces, sprinklings of sugar, pinches of salt, dashes of Shaoxing wine and slivers of ginger, spring onion and garlic, I create hundreds of tried and tested dishes. I always use the freshest ingredients of the highest quality. And that will never change.

So you see, there's no celebrity to sell here. Just experience from some fifty years of kitchen life.

Michael Peng:
A few words about my father

When I was asked to write a few words about my father I wasn't too keen on doing it. For starters, I don't really write. More worrying is the fact that my father is a bit of an enigma. After all these years growing up and now working in the restaurant with him, I'm still trying to figure him out. The only thing I'm sure of is that he is a gifted cook with an unflinching belief in traditional Chinese values.

I suppose this is reflected in his cooking style; it is steeped in tradition but you can't compartmentalise it. If I had to describe him in three words it would be: focused, uncompromising, traditionalist. He is very much a staunch believer in Chinese culture, and a man of few words. He talks only about food and the restaurant. He lives and breathes food and when he does express himself, he expresses himself the only way he knows how, through cooking. I don't think we have ever sat down and had a personal conversation, it is just not in his character. He's coy about the past and rarely expresses his feelings, but this is a common trait among his generation. Everything I know about him centres on cooking and the restaurant.

If anything, becoming a dad myself has brought my father and me closer together. It's surreal to see my children playing in the restaurant now, like I did all those years ago, and it not only illustrates how quickly time has passed but how proud I am of what he has achieved.

It was clear to me from a young age that he is a creative, tireless chef who never stops and is never satisfied. His is the stereotypical immigrant story about a couple who came to the UK with nothing but the desire to better their lives.

My father often tells me, 'talk is cheap and nothing substitutes hard work and a strong work ethic'. Back when he first started he didn't have a day off for over ten years. Even at nearly seventy years old, he is never idle and will still put in a shift and a half; when the rest of the chefs are taking a break, he continues with the prep. It keeps him young and he will only stop when he is physically unable to do it any more.

His values have been instilled into me and my sisters over the years. We were all expected to pull our weight as youngsters and we always had to make a contribution towards the business. As much as we resented working through weekends and holidays, greeting and serving customers or washing the wok in the basement, it made us realise how difficult it was back then for our parents, which is not a bad thing.

Customers often ask me why the restaurant is called Hunan. They say, 'Your father's cooking is not Hunanese?' That's true. It's another quirk in his personality. When the restaurant first opened he served dishes mainly from the Hunan province, such as double-cooked pork, and some of these original dishes are still being offered to customers today. But over the years my father has adapted and incorporated the other styles of cooking he had learnt before he opened Hunan. His cooking style is a mixture of Hunanese, Taiwanese, Cantonese, Sichuan and Northern Chinese (dong bei). The restaurant was named in honour of his first mentor who taught him Hunanese cooking and he will never change the name.

My father doesn't do change. He tells me all the time that change is bad and made me promise not to alter the kooky layout of the restaurant so to this day the interior and décor of the restaurant remains the same. My grandfather laid out the plans for the restaurant according to feng shui which plays a big part in our lives. There are lots of idioms and behaviours that we adhere to. When sweeping the floor we always sweep inwards, not outwards towards the direction of the front door. If you do this, it means you are sweeping good fortune away and out of the restaurant.

The way our chefs work has changed very little over the years, how we operate day to day is the same. We tried to bring in a computer system but it just didn't work because we don't have a menu. As a result, we still have to write the orders by hand. It's time consuming and sometimes frustrating but that's how my father likes it. The biggest change to have happened to the restaurant in thirty years is that we are now open six instead of seven days a week.

Despite having countless opportunities to expand, my father has never wanted to. He's very hands on in the restaurant and wants to be there every day, meeting, greeting and cooking. He used to work the front of house in a suit and would then rush downstairs, whip on an apron, make a dish and then whizz back up again, plate in hand. It was relentless.

When the restaurant first opened in 1982 the intention was never to have 'a no menu policy'. There was a short à la carte menu with about forty dishes on it and a 'leave it to us menu'. My father sometimes used to 'force' different dishes on to customers which didn't go down too well. A customer would order sweet and sour pork and dad would serve them a completely different dish. He would try and explain that they should try something different, he wanted to educate them.

Back in the Eighties most Chinese restaurants in the UK were Cantonese and he wanted to let people know there was more to Chinese cuisine. However, the reality was that many customers were horrified that the chef had the audacity to give them something they hadn't ordered. Fortunately we also had some customers who were bowled over by the different cuisine, and these customers have been coming back ever since.

My most vivid recollections of the restaurant as a child were of lots of customers walking out and lots of shouting on Pimlico Road. My father is not the type to hold back. At that time he had more sceptics than fans so business was tough and we almost folded. But in typical fashion, he stuck to his guns. As word spread and customers started to put more trust in him, evenings would go by where no one ordered from the menu and eventually, due to the lack of demand, he decided to just stop doing it. It was down to his sheer persistence, belief that he knew best and the fact that he wanted to share his knowledge with the customers that the menu-less set up remained.

There is no question that after thirty-one years he is still a big personality in the restaurant. He has been described as arrogant and bolshy, which is true to an extent but one thing is for sure, he won't change a single thing.

You could say this book is a culmination of his life's work. He has been wanting to do this for a long time. I recall our first meeting to talk about the book. My father said 'I don't care about the money' which is probably not the wisest thing to say. But in that split second he had already made up his mind and knew what he wanted to do. This is an insight into my father.

A few thoughts on...

Flavour

The vast array of flavours in Chinese cuisine is not easy to achieve, even if you have all of the ingredients. Although we do a lot of things by eye in the kitchen, the right balance comes from years of experience and, of course, tasting everything.

That said, it's important to remember that these recipes are every bit as much yours as they are mine when you get to the kitchen. With that in mind, the quantities given should only be used as a guide and you can use the quantities that you feel comfortable with – not everything needs to be as salty or spicy as I like it.

The easiest way to achieve your preferred combination is by mixing all of the ingredients for sauces, dressings and marinades in a bowl before applying to the rest of the ingredients. Here, before you start the cooking, you will have an opportunity to taste it and decide if the flavours are right for your palate.

At the restaurant, we would typically serve between 16-18 courses for a meal, each one a morsel of deliciousness, ripe for the palate. This is perfect for us, because it means that our guests can have so many different flavour experiences in one sitting.

In China we have always eaten nose-to-tail and believe in making the most of the entire animal. Offal isn't to everyone's liking but at Hunan we transform the forgotten bits of the animal into delicious, aromatic dishes that even the most squeamish diners enjoy. Try the recipes for tongue and ear salad on p.160 and ox tongue with marmalade on p.150 and I'm sure you will change your mind!

Be mindful of three things.

Firstly that the main ingredients themselves will add flavour to the finished dish and also take flavour away, so make sure the flavourings complement the natural saltiness, sweetness, acidity and bitterness of the main ingredient. For example, a fermented ingredient like preserved vegetables will need less salt than something like chicken, and a relatively flavourless addition like noodles will need more flavour to be imparted from the sauces and marinades.

The second consideration is how you will eat the dish. At Hunan, we don't serve rice or noodles until the end of the meal so the dishes are relatively less salty than you might otherwise find them. Depending on whether you serve the dish with or without rice, you may need to adjust the flavours accordingly.

And finally, remember that any liquids used in the cooking will reduce during the cooking process, especially in the hot and fast cooking of stir-fries where water evaporates quickly. It's advisable therefore to add a little water or stock to a sauce before cooking to account for the evaporation during cooking.

Temperature

There are three cooking temperatures, each used for different types of cooking.

Wei huo (微火)

The lowest of the three is called *wei huo*. This is best for slow-cooking dishes such as stews and for more delicate ingredients like fresh tofu. Ideally, use a casserole dish for slow-cooking to allow even distribution of heat.

Zhong huo (中火)

Medium heat, or *zhong huo*, is suitable for some meats, seafood and noodles. This is when the ingredients take slightly longer to cook, so you need a lower temperature to prevent burning.

Da huo (大火)

Da huo is the highest of the three temperatures and commonly used for stir-frying anything that needs fast cooking, or that must be eaten straight after leaving the pan, for best results. It's only achievable with a steel wok. However, there's a certain fragrant freshness that comes from stir-frying in a really hot wok that can't be replicated by any other method of cooking. That's what the Chinese often refer to as *gou wei* (锅味), or 'taste of the wok'.

When cooking at high temperature at home, make sure the oil in the pan is almost smoking before adding salt and then the rest of your ingredients. Like with deep-frying, make sure your ingredients are completely dry, otherwise you may be surprised by the amount of scalding oil that will splash back.

The wok

The most commonly used piece of equipment in the Chinese kitchen is the steel wok. Its shape keeps the food in the pan during stir-frying and helps the food to cook quickly, it's easy to clean between dishes, and the highest cooking temperatures are only achievable with a steel wok. Its large surface area means that ingredients can cook in moments on an even heat.

The steamer

Always use a bamboo steamer, as it allows the steam to circulate during cooking. With metal and plastic steamers, you get too much condensation forming at the top.

To use your bamboo steamer, set a pan of water to simmer on the hob, and take a steamer which will sit on top of the pan where the lid would otherwise be. We usually steam the dish in whatever plate it will be served on, so make sure your plates are steam-proof before using them in the steamer.

Vinegar

When cooking on a high heat, a small amount of vinegar added right at the end of cooking, just before the stir-fry leaves the wok, helps to lift a dish. It's a last-minute addition as prolonged cooking will alter the flavour of the vinegar and therefore the dish.

The vinegar will also help to soften any vegetables in the stir-fry as it replaces the water that has evaporated during cooking. This way, the vegetables in a stir-fry stay tender, crunchy and aromatic.

Store cupboard

Chinese cuisine is all about the balance of flavours and ingredients. It's never as simple as adding salt or butter to a dish. Instead, it's much more about blending the nuances in the flavours of different ingredients until you find the point where everything works in harmony and the best part of each ingredient shines through.

In the Hunan kitchen, we have a variety of store-cupboard ingredients – fresh, fermented, wet and dried – to help us achieve the point of perfection in our cooking! They lend us limitless possibilities. Some ingredients, like salt and sugar, go into almost every dish; others, like miso paste and Chinese five spice, in just a few. But each one is important for the layer of flavour that it brings to the dish, and each is the best quality we can get.

For the home kitchen, you really don't need to stock up on a huge number of ingredients and you can make substitutions to achieve the flavours you're looking for. But to make authentic, unique dishes, always have the following staples at your fingertips:

Fresh

Ginger
薑

Ginger is used in Chinese culture for its medicinal properties as well as its flavour. It's almost always fresh but you can freeze it if you have too much. The spicy perfume is especially important in seafood dishes but its earthy flavour also works well for meat. For these recipes the ginger can be sliced, minced, shredded or simply crushed depending on the length of time of cooking. For dressings, it's always used with vinegar.

Spring onions
蔥

Spring onions are used during cooking as well as as a raw garnish. They can be cut into medallions (or 'coins'), on the diagonal, shredded or just in lengths.

The stalk of the spring onion has stronger flavours and is perfect for soups as it maintains clarity, but the green of the plant adds great colour for contrast in stir-fries. Spring onion also has the wonderful property of being able to remove the sometimes unsavoury smell of offal and seafood.

Garlic
大蒜

We use garlic in many ways at Hunan but its flavour can be overpowering, so we always use it sparingly.

Whole garlic cloves, with skin on or off, are used in marinades and soups. Sliced garlic is added to stir-fries to provide flavour and sometimes for aesthetic purposes, and minced garlic is used to flavour dressings and sauces.

In some dishes, we use garlic juice instead of garlic cloves. It's made simply by soaking minced garlic in water, before straining. The concentrated allium notes of the garlic juice often work better than garlic cloves in marinades.

Fresh red chillies
新鮮紅辣椒

Fresh red chillies appear most often as a garnish because of their striking colour. In certain dishes, they are added as they have a more subtle spicy flavour than the chilli sauces and don't have the smokiness of the dried red chillies.

Chillies are available in all sorts of colours and you can always use the variety that you're comfortable with. For a little less spice, simply remove the seeds.

Fermented

Fermented bean curd
豆腐乳

There are lots of different kinds of fermented bean curds but the two main ones are the red fermented bean curd and the white fermented bean curd.

Red fermented bean curd (*hong fu ru*, 紅腐乳) is made by fermenting bean curd (tofu) with red yeast rice, which gives the bean curd its distinctive colour but also a more concentrated flavour than white fermented bean curd. It adds umami flavours to marinades and sauces but also imparts a fantastic red colour to the finished dish.

White fermented bean curd (*dou fu ru*, 豆腐乳) is normally used for vegetables and dips. Red fermented bean curd is used in roasting and grilling and for cooking sauces. Both are ready to eat and are great with Chinese mantou or congee (Chinese rice porridge).

Wet

Soy sauce – dark and light
老抽和生抽

Many of you will already know there are two different types of soy sauce – dark (*lao chou*, 抽) and light (*sheng chou*, 生抽). What you might not know however, is how they differ and when to use them. As a guide, dark soy sauce is darker in colour than light soy sauce. Light soy sauce is used to flavour food while dark soy sauce is used more to impart colour.

Stock
高湯

One of the most widely used ingredients in the kitchen is stock. It goes in soups, noodles, stir-fries and sauces. Just about everything really.

Chicken stock is often used as it gives a great depth of flavour but isn't too overpowering for lighter dishes. In most cases, if you don't have stock to hand, you can always use water. Sometimes, in things like soups, it's very important to have a good stock for the base. You can substitute chicken stock for vegetable stock if you are feeding vegetarians.

Sesame oil
香油

Sesame oil is nutty and aromatic. It can overpower food if it is used in the cooking process but it's perfect for adding interest to a dish at the end of cooking.

As it's quite dense in both aroma and texture, it's important to taste the other ingredients of a dish before you add the sesame oil to ensure that you have the right balance of flavours.

Shaoxing wine
绍興酒

Shaoxing wine is an aromatic alcohol made from fermented rice and is used throughout Chinese cooking. It has an inherent sweetness so sometimes sherry can make a good substitute but it's indispensable for adding complexity to light and fresh dishes such as steamed fish.

Deep-fried shallots and shallot oil
炸蔥頭和紅蔥油

There's a word in Chinese called *xiang* (香). It embodies fragrance and aroma, a sort of umami for the nose. Deep fried shallots and shallot oil are both added to dishes for the xiang that they bring to the table. Deep fried shallots add a softly crunchy texture while the shallot oil, a by-product of making the deep fried shallots, is perfect for drizzling over finished dishes and for cooking when its heady perfume is needed.

Dried

Sichuan peppercorns
花椒

Sichuan peppercorns are now a familiar ingredient in Western cuisine. They produce a delicately hot, but distinctively numbing sensation on your tongue. Their smell and taste is quite different from that of other peppercorns and they feature prominently in many cuisines, not just Sichuan.

The peppercorns can be used either whole or ground. Uncooked whole Sichuan peppercorns are naturally fragrant but become even more so when heated during cooking. They add just a hint of pepperiness to dishes but you can leave them out if you want to avoid the numbing sensation on your tongue.

Ground Sichuan peppercorns are made by first toasting the peppercorns in a dry pan until they begin to release their fragrance, before crushing them. The result is small flecks of pepper, rather than a finely milled powder, that can be easily added to dressings.

Add some salt to toasted, crushed Sichuan peppercorns and you will have *jiao yan* (椒盐), the basic flavouring in dishes such as dry-fried prawns.

Dried chillies
乾辣椒

We have used two forms of dried chillies in these recipes – whole dried red chillies and chilli flakes.

Whole dried red chillies are added to stir-fries to provide colour contrast and a hint of heat. Chilli flakes are used to flavour dishes and also to make chilli sauces and oils.

Ground pepper
胡椒粉

In Chinese cuisine, ground white pepper is used more frequently than ground black pepper. While both offer subtle peppery notes, ground white pepper is the more delicate of the two and works better in fish, seafood and chicken dishes. Black pepper is more robust and works well with stronger-tasting meats such as lamb and beef.

Chinese five spice
五香粉

Chinese five spice is a very finely ground mixture of star anise, cloves, cinnamon, Sichuan peppercorns and fennel seeds. It's great for bringing fried foods to life and for certain sauces when you just want a hint of spice.

Star anise and cinnamon
八角和肉桂

Star anise and cinnamon are almost always used together in Chinese cuisine because they work well together and are quite harmonious for most dishes. It's because of this that as a spice category, they are called *da liao* (大料) or big flavours.

There's no set occasion for when they are used in Chinese cookery. Normally they are used for meats as they can be too overpowering for vegetables, although some people like the taste they bring to a dish.

Cornflour
玉米粉

Cornflour is so versatile in the kitchen. It's used to dust ingredients before frying so that they are extra crispy. Slaked cornflour (roughly three parts water to one part cornflour) helps to thicken sauces. It's used to coat meats to help them stay tender by sealing in the moisture. And of course, cornflour is great for helping fillings to bind together.

Salt and sugar
鹽和糖

Salt and sugar really need no introduction as ingredients – they are used to add flavour and balance. Sugar, especially, is used to address the acidity from vinegars and from the natural acidity of the ingredients.

The salt used in this book is plain cooking salt while the sugar is granulated white sugar or, where specified, palm sugar.

In addition to the key ingredients, there are a few others that are worth having in your store cupboard, or at least knowing about. If you can't find them in your usual supermarket, you can obtain them from Chinese stores, supermarkets or online stockists.

Miso paste
味噌醬

Miso paste is often regarded as a Japanese ingredient but is actually very similar to the fermented tofu used in Chinese cuisine. While fermented tofu is made with soya beans and tends to be saltier, with a soft curd texture, miso paste, when made with rice, is drier and sweeter. Adding Shaoxing wine and fresh ginger will help bring it to life and inject a wonderful aroma while vinegar will balance its natural sweetness.

Tian mian jiang
甜麵醬

Tian mian jiang, or sweet flour paste, is made from fermented flour and soya beans. It's similar to Hoisin sauce but is darker, sweeter and has greater complexity in flavour. If you can't find it, you can always substitute it with Hoisin sauce.

Sesame seeds
芝麻

Sesame seeds, while aromatic when toasted, are mostly used as a garnish. In some dishes, like the spinach parcels, they also add texture.

Red yeast rice
红麴

Red yeast rice is created as a result of rice being combined with a special kind of yeast. The earthy flavours are subtle but it does add a vibrant red colour to dishes so it's often used as a natural colouring.

Jiu qu
酒麴

Jiu qu, sometimes translated to wine rice, is an alcoholic rice product where the rice used in the fermentation process is left in the alcohol. It doesn't have a strong alcohol content but it's very aromatic and has a hint of sweetness and acidity.

Red chilli oil
辣椒油

Clear red chilli oil is used both as a garnish, its vibrant red colour offering contrast, and also to impart fiery heat. Ready-made varieties are widely available but chilli oil is also simple enough to make. Just add hot oil to chilli flakes, and allow to cool before straining.

Chilli sauce

Chilli aficionados will know there are lots of different chilli sauces. Aside from the obvious differences in heat, there are also different levels of acidity, sweetness, saltiness and sometimes savouriness which in turn match different dishes. For example, the sweeter ones work better for Cantonese-style dishes and the spicier ones work better in stir-fries.

There are two main chilli sauces used at Hunan, both made in-house. For certain dishes, we also use ready-made chilli sauces like sweet chilli sauce or chilli bean sauce which adds additional flavours and textures.

Red chilli sauce
紅辣椒醬

The vibrantly red chilli sauce is the less spicy of the two house chilli sauces and its flavours are more rounded. The tomato purée in the sauce gives it stunning structure which helps to carry the chilli flavours through. See page 250.

Sichuan chilli sauce
川味辣椒醬

The Sichuan chilli sauce is almost too dark to be recognisable, until you taste it. The toasted chilli flakes creates a dense smoky base for the fiery chilli oil. To top it off, there's the numbing sensation left on your tongue by the Sichuan peppercorns. It's a staple for Sichuan influenced dishes and easily allows the addition of spring onion and ginger for a fresh tasting dressing. See page 252.

Vinegar

Vinegar is used to add acidity to almost every stir-fry dish right at the end, just before the wok leaves the heat. The punchy freshness it adds helps to lift the flavour and aroma of the dish.

There are several different types of vinegars, creating different flavour profiles. It's certainly not just the standard Chinese black vinegar – though of course that's used too.

White wine vinegar
白葡萄酒醋

White wine vinegar is the most widely used. It works in dishes with seafood, chicken, duck and vegetables and in many soups. It has a light profile so adds acidity without adding other flavours.

Chinese black vinegar
中國黑醋

Chinese black vinegar is so distinctive that it's rarely used. Its intensity and complexity of flavours is great in marinades but can be overpowering in stir-fries.

Red wine vinegar
紅葡萄酒醋

Red wine vinegar works best in dishes featuring beef, lamb and gamey meats. It has a more rounded acidity which lends weight to a dish. So while white wine vinegar might be overpowered by red meats, red wine vinegar will sit quite comfortably and add freshness to the dish.

All about oil

What kind of oil?

At Hunan I cook with vegetable oil and never with animal fats
whether I am stir-frying, pan-frying or deep-frying. It's much
healthier and also gives the dish a fresh, clean flavour.

I do sometimes use othcr flavourless oils such as rapeseed oil
as long as they can withstand the heat of the wok or deep-fat
fryer. Sesame oil should only be used as a flavouring and never
for cooking.

How to deep-fry safely?

There are many safety concerns around deep-frying. As anyone who has deep-fried anything will know, unless your ingredients and utensils are completely dry, hot oil will splash out of the pan. Dab any remaining liquids off ingredients with a paper towel and shake off any excess batter.

The best way to achieve the right temperature when deep-frying is to let the oil heat up from cold. It will begin to come to temperature when the oil starts to move around in the pan unaided and this is when you should test for temperature. You can do this by using a temperature probe. If you don't have one, use a tester piece. Place a small tester piece of your ingredients into the oil carefully. It should bubble and float easily on its own but not turn brown within 10 seconds. If it does, the oil is too hot and you should allow it to cool by taking it off the heat.

When you put the item to be deep-fried into the oil, make sure you use a dry spatula or slotted spoon. Gently slide the ingredient into the oil and away from you. You should cover your arms to give yourself maximum protection from burning.

When taking things out of the hot oil, turn the heat off from under the pan and use a dry slotted spoon to remove your items to a plate.

Poultry
家禽

Chicken in spicy sauce
椒麻雞柳

This dish works brilliantly as a snack because it's simple and straightforward. Perfect, in fact, as a nibble to accompany a glass of beer.

Heat a good glug of oil in a wok, until it's nearly smoking.

Coat the chicken slices with the cornflour and then the beaten egg.

Deep-fry the chicken slices in the hot oil for a minute or so. When they begin to turn golden, remove from the oil and set aside. Discard the oil.

Mix all the ingredients for the sauce in a bowl and adjust for seasoning. When you are happy with the flavour, pour the sauce into the wok and heat through.

Return the chicken to the wok to warm through.

Season with salt and sugar to taste before serving.

Makes 4 portions

1 chicken breast, thinly sliced

2 tbsp cornflour, to coat

1 egg, beaten, to coat

vegetable or rapeseed oil, for deep-frying

For the sauce:

1 tbsp Sichuan chilli sauce (see recipe on page 252)

2 tsp white wine vinegar

1 tsp soy sauce

2 tsp shallot oil

1 fresh red chilli, finely sliced

1 spring onion, finely sliced

½ tsp tian mian jiang

2 tsp water

salt and sugar, to taste

Spicy chicken wings
鹽焗雞翅

This salty and aromatic dish is another great companion to beer. Marinating the chicken for a short time beforehand helps the flavours seep through while keeping the meat delicate enough so it doesn't fight with the spicy dressing.

Mix all the ingredients for the marinade together in a bowl, add the chicken and leave to marinate for 5 minutes.

Heat a griddle or griddle pan, and slowly cook the wings on a medium heat without adding any oil. You want the skin to crisp up evenly but the meat to be cooked through. This should take around 20 minutes.

Meanwhile, mix all the dressing ingredients together in a bowl. Adjust the seasoning.

When the wings are ready, spoon the dressing over them and sprinkle with sesame seeds before serving.

Makes 4 portions

4 chicken wings, skin on

For the marinade:

4 tbsp Shaoxing wine

2 tbsp garlic juice

2 tsp Sichuan peppercorns

1 tsp salt

For the dressing:

2 tsp chilli oil

½ fresh red chilli, finely sliced

1 spring onion, finely sliced

To garnish:

sesame seeds

Dry-fried chicken
乾煸雞柳

Chicken cooked this way is very crispy and fragrant without being too dry. It's another great nibble to enjoy with an ice-cold beer.

Coat the chicken strips with cornflour.

Heat a good glug of oil in a wok until it's nearly smoking.

Deep-fry the coated chicken breast on a high heat until golden-brown.

In a clean wok, dry-fry the chillies, garlic and spring onions until they become fragrant. Add the chicken to the pan, season with the salt and crushed Sichuan peppercorns, then stir through to warm before serving.

Makes 4 portions

1 chicken breast, cut into thin strips

2 tbsp cornflour, to coat

2 tsp oil

3 fresh red chillies, sliced

3 garlic cloves, minced

vegetable oil for deep-frying

3 spring onions, thinly sliced

salt and crushed Sichuan peppercorns, to season

Sichuan-style stir-fry chicken
川溜雞柳

Deep-fried chicken is really dry so when you add a sauce to it, it will soak up all of the juices and flavours immediately. That means you will need to work quickly once you've added the chicken to the sauce to make sure that the chicken is still crispy but full of flavour when it reaches the table. This is a dish that will not wait!

Coat the strips of chicken first with cornflour and then with beaten egg to create a light batter coating around the meat.

Heat a generous amount of oil in a wok and deep-fry the meat on a high heat for 5 minutes or so until the chicken turns golden. Remove to kitchen paper to drain, and set aside.

Meanwhile, mix all the sauce ingredients together in a bowl, and adjust the seasoning. Add to a clean wok or pan and heat through.

When the sauce is ready, add the chicken strips and quickly stir through. Remove to serving plates, add the chopped spring onion and serve straight away.

Makes 4 portions

1 chicken breast, cut into thin strips

cornflour, to coat

1 egg, beaten, to coat

For the sauce:

1 tbsp Sichuan chilli sauce
(see recipe on page 252)

1 tsp crushed Sichuan peppercorns

1 garlic clove, minced

½ tbsp white wine vinegar

2 tbsp water

1 tbsp cooking oil

1 tsp sugar

pinch of salt

To serve:

1 spring onion, roughly chopped

Stuffed chicken wings
糯米雞翅

The juxtaposition of the crispy outside and yielding inside makes these wings positively moreish, and they are great as a snack with drinks before dinner.

Cook the sticky rice according to the instructions on the pack, and set aside.

Soak the dried shrimps and shiitake mushrooms in some stock to rehydrate them. Once they have softened, drain and finely chop along with the Chinese sausage.

In a wok, heat a little oil and stir fry the shrimp, mushroom, sausage and rice with the soy sauce until well combined.

Make the wings into drummers by stripping back the flesh along the bones, ensuring that one end of the wing is still attached to the bone. Make sure you keep the wing meat whole so you can stuff it. Dust inside and outside with a little cornflour.

Stuff the wings with the filling and wrap tightly in cling film.

Set your bamboo steamer on top of a pan of simmering water and steam the parcels on a plate for 5 minutes until the meat is cooked through.

Mix a little of the cornflour with some water to make a light batter. Unwrap the steamed chicken wings carefully and lightly coat with the batter.

Deep-fry the stuffed wings until golden.

Once the wings are ready, slice open diagonally and serve on top of a bed of shredded lettuce and dress with Sichuan chilli pepper sauce and deep-fried shallots.

Makes 6 portions

6 chicken wings, upper lengths only

cornflour to coat

For the filling:

40g dried shrimps

4 dried shiitake mushrooms

2 lengths Chinese sausage

200g cooked sticky rice

2 tbsp light soy sauce

To serve:

Sichuan chilli sauce, deep-fried shallots and shredded lettuce

Chicken with baby olives
破布子溜雞柳

Baby olives are preserved with their stones intact so you have to be careful when eating this dish as the seeds are inedible. If you remove the seeds before cooking, the baby olives will disintegrate. They are essential to the flavour of this dish because they give a dry sweetness and add a savoury note not found in other olives. If you can't get hold of baby olives, ordinary olives will be fine, just make sure that you remove the stones and cut them into quarters.

Coat the chicken breast with cornflour and beaten egg before shallow frying in a wok of hot oil for about 1 minute. As the colour of the meat begins to change, remove from the oil and set aside.

In the same wok, add the stock, baby olives, ginger, chilli and a little cooking oil and heat through. As the sauce begins to reduce, add the Shaoxing wine and return the chicken to the wok. Taste and adjust for seasoning.

Cook for a further minute and adjust seasoning.

Just before serving, stir through the white wine vinegar and sesame oil.

Makes 4 portions

1 chicken breast, finely sliced

1 beaten egg to coat

cornflour to coat

1 tbsp stock

2 tbsp baby olives

2½ cm ginger, finely sliced

2 red chillies, finely sliced

2 tsp Shaoxing wine

1 tsp white wine vinegar

2 tsp sesame oil

salt and sugar to taste

Chicken in pineapple and bitter melon sauce
鳳梨苦瓜雞

The unique combination of pineapple and bitter melon, two seemingly opposite flavours, is a perfect example of yin and yang harmonising. The yin and yang refers to the effects of food on the body – pineapple falls into the yang category while the bitter melon is the yin. The balance is a delicate one and requires slow and careful cooking. If you cook the pineapple for too long, its sugars will begin to burn, and the longer you cook the bitter melon, the more bitter it will become.

First, make the sauce by heating the pineapple and bitter melon with the stock, and simmer gently for about 20 minutes. The sauce is ready when you can break down the pineapple and melon pieces with the back of a spoon.

Meanwhile, in a bowl, mix the chicken mince with the spring onion, water chestnuts and the 2 teaspoons of cornflour. Season with a pinch of salt.

Form the mixture into walnut-sized balls and place on a tray lined with cornflour. Once you have made all the balls, shake the tray to dust all the balls with cornflour.

Mix the beaten egg with the teaspoon of water, and blend. Dip the chicken balls in the egg mixture, then shake to remove the excess egg.

Heat a little oil in a wok, and shallow-fry the chicken balls. When the edges begin to take on colour, turn the balls over to cook the other side.

When both sides are golden, remove the chicken balls to a separate, dry pan and cook both sides to crisp up the edges.

When the pineapple and bitter melon from the sauce have softened, remove from the heat and add the ginger, spring onion, chilli, sugar, vinegar and a little salt. Taste for seasoning before adding the slaked cornflour, return to the heat and cook to thicken.

When the chicken balls are ready, cut in half and put on a serving plate. Pour the sauce on top, and serve.

Makes 4 portions

200g chicken mince, from thighs

½ spring onion, finely chopped

2 water chestnuts, minced

2 tsp cornflour, to bind, plus more for dusting

pinch of salt

1 egg, beaten, to coat

1 tsp water

vegetable or rapeseed oil, for frying

For the sauce:

25g pineapple, finely diced

25g bitter melon, finely diced

100ml chicken stock

1 cm piece fresh ginger, thinly sliced

1 spring onion stalk, thinly sliced

¼ red chilli, thinly sliced

1 tsp sugar

1 tsp white wine vinegar

1 tsp slaked cornflour

salt, to taste

Miso chicken
味噌煨雞

To balance the dry sweetness of the miso paste, add Shaoxing wine and ginger for aroma and vinegar for acidity. Chicken breast is a must for this dish because the grain of the meat helps to carry through the subtleties in the flavours.

Make the sauce first by mixing the miso paste, Shaoxing wine, chicken stock, soy sauce, cornflour, sugar and ground white pepper together in a bowl. Adjust for taste, adding salt and sugar as necessary, then add the ginger and spring onions, and set aside.

Cut the chicken breast diagonally to get wide thin slices. You can get about six slices from one chicken breast. Tenderise it by lightly piercing with a knife. Season the chicken with a little salt before dusting with the cornflour.

Add some oil to the wok and heat until just beginning to smoke. Coat the chicken with the beaten egg and add straight to the hot wok. When the chicken is just beginning to brown, flip it over and cook the other side.

When the chicken is brown on both sides, remove from the wok and set aside.

In the same wok, add the mixed sauce and cook through. Add the remaining chicken stock and slaked cornflour and warm through.

Return the chicken to the wok to cook with the sauce briefly. Add the vinegar and sesame oil just before serving.

Plate up either in individual portions or as one large plate. Arrange the Chinese cabbage on the plate or plates, place the chicken on top and drizzle with the sauce. Garnish with chopped chillies before serving.

Makes 6 portions

1 chicken breast

pinch of salt

pinch of sugar

½ tbsp cornflour

1 egg, beaten

300ml chicken stock

1 tsp slaked cornflour

1 tsp white wine vinegar

1 tsp sesame oil

vegetable oil, for frying

For the sauce:

½ tbsp miso paste

1 tbsp Shaoxing wine

1½ tbsp chicken stock

1 tsp light soy sauce

1 tsp slaked cornflour

pinch of sugar and ground white pepper

1 cm piece fresh ginger, minced

½ spring onion, finely chopped

To serve:

1 Chinese cabbage leaf blanched and refreshed

To garnish:

Chopped red chillies

Lotus root stuffed with chicken
酒釀蓮藕雞

The lotus root becomes very crunchy when cooked and the red fermented bean curd gives it an extra aroma. The jiu qu wine rice adds a unique sweet and sour flavour with just a hint of alcohol. If you can't find it, use Shaoxing wine as a substitute.

Peel the lotus roots and cut into 5mm thick medallions. You need about four slices for the amount of filling here, two slices per portion. This will vary depending on the size of your lotus root.

Make the filling by mixing all the ingredients together in a bowl.

Sandwich a portion of filling between each lotus root slice to 1 cm thick. Make sure the filling goes right to the edge of the parcel but without it spilling out.

Coat the whole of each parcel with cornflour.

Coat the sides of the parcels, where the filling is exposed, with the beaten egg and cover with sesame seeds.

Heat a good amount of oil in a wok and deep-fry the parcels on a high heat until golden all over. This will take around 5 minutes.

Meanwhile, make the sauce by mixing all the ingredients together in a bowl. Adjust the seasoning before gently warming through in a pan.

When the parcels are cooked, slice them diagonally.

Serve on top of a bed of shredded lettuce and drizzle the warmed sauce on top. Garnish with chilli, spring onion and ginger.

Makes 4 portions

2 lotus roots

cornflour, to coat

1 egg, beaten, to coat

sesame seeds, to coat

oil, for deep-frying

For the filling:

4 tbsp chicken mince

4 tsp red fermented bean curd

2 garlic cloves, minced

2 tsp cornflour

salt and sugar, to taste

For the sauce:

2 tbsp red fermented bean curd

2 tsp jiu qu rice wine

1 garlic clove, minced

1 tsp Chinese five spice

pinch of sugar

2 tbsp chicken stock

To serve:

shredded lettuce

To garnish:

chopped chilli, spring onion and fresh ginger

' The lotus root becomes very crunchy when cooked and the red fermented bean curd gives it an extra aroma '

Chicken and water chestnut parcels

馬蹄雞球

This dish is really crunchy but also slightly sweet because the main component is the water chestnut. The sauce is put on the parcel at the last minute or served on the side to maintain the mouthfeel of this dish.

Make the filling by mixing all of the filling ingredients except the chicken mince together in a bowl. Adjust to taste before adding the chicken mince.

Slice the water chestnut into fine slices. You need about 4 from each chestnut.

Sandwich a little of the the filling between 2 slices of water chestnut, about a centimetre in height.

Dust each of the parcels with cornflour. Dab with a little water if not sticking together.

Roll the filling side of the parcel in egg and cover with sesame seeds.

Heat a generous amount of oil in a wok until almost smoking.

Deep-fry the parcels at a high heat until golden.

Meanwhile, make a sauce by warming all of the finishing sauce ingredients in a very small pan. When the parcels are ready, serve each one on top of a lettuce leaf. Dress with the warmed sauce and garnish with a coriander leaf.

Makes 4 portions

2 water chestnuts

cornflour to coat

1 beaten egg to coat

sesame seeds to coat

For the filling:

3 spring onions, roughly chopped

1 clove garlic, minced

1 tsp cornflour

salt and black pepper

100g minced chicken

To finish:

1 tbsp sweet chilli sauce

1 tsp light soy sauce

½ tsp red wine vinegar

½ tsp sesame oil

1 cm ginger, finely sliced

To serve:
lettuce leaf

To garnish:
coriander leaves

Whole stuffed aubergine
湘味茄龍

A whole stuffed aubergine is really versatile. It lends itself to red-hot chilli sauce or a miso sauce with ginger and shallot. We always use Chinese aubergines at Hunan, they are longer and have a lower water content than standard aubergines. Here I've used a fermented bean sauce to play on the natural colour of the cooked aubergine.

Slice an aubergine, at an angle, most of the way down so that it remains whole but opens up like a fan.

Make the filling by mixing together all of the ingredients for the filling in a bowl. Cook a little off to taste for seasoning.

Stuff the gaps in the aubergine with the filling, like a sandwich, and coat the whole aubergine with cornflour.

Heat a good glug of oil in a wok until it's almost smoking. Deep-fry the whole aubergine for about 10 minutes until it's golden.

Meanwhile, make the sauce by mixing all of the ingredients for the sauce in a small pan and heating through. Add more stock to the sauce if necessary to reach a thick but runny mixture.

When the aubergine is ready, drizzle the sauce over the top and serve.

Makes 8 portions

1 whole aubergine, about 300g

cornflour to coat

For the filling:

100g minced chicken

3 sprigs spring onion, roughly chopped

1 tsp minced garlic

1 tsp cornflour

salt and pepper to season

For the sauce:

1 tbsp tian mian jiang

1 tbsp fermented bean paste

1 tbsp Sichuan chilli sauce

garlic clove, minced

1 roughly chopped spring onion

50ml stock

Duck and spinach parcels
翡翠鴨脯

This dish is stunning to look at and great to taste. After all, apart from salad, how many other dishes do you see this vibrant green? To keep it vibrant, make sure you warm the spinach juice very gently.

Bring a large pan of water to the boil with a teaspoon of salt. Add the duck and turn the heat down to a simmer. Cook the duck for about 20 minutes before removing from the pan and cooling.

When the duck is cold, cut into 1 cm-thick slices. You should have about 6 slices. For each slice, cut two-thirds of the way down the slice so you have a pocket to stuff the filling into.

Poach the spinach in hot water for about 1 minute until the leaves have softened.

Drain the spinach and blend in a blender or food processor until smooth.

Pass the mixture through a fine sieve placed over a bowl to separate the juice and the pulp. Set aside.

In a bowl, mix the spinach pulp with the chicken mince, ginger and water chestnuts.

Stuff the duck breast pockets with the filling to form parcels.

Add a little oil to a wok and warm until nearly smoking.

Coat the entire duck parcel with cornflour and then with beaten egg before shallow-frying in the oil on a high heat until golden.

Meanwhile, make the sauce by heating the spinach juice with the teaspoon of cooking oil and salt and sugar to taste. As it warms through, add the slaked cornflour. Cook until the sauce has thickened. Just before serving, add the vinegar and stir through.

When the duck is ready pour the sauce over the parcels. Garnish with shredded chilli.

Makes 6 portions

1 tsp salt

1 large duck breast, skin on

100g spinach

For the filling:

50g chicken mince

1 cm piece of fresh minced ginger

2 water chestnuts, minced

cornflour, to coat

1 egg, beaten, to coat

For the sauce:

1 tsp cooking oil

salt and sugar, to taste

½ tsp slaked cornflour

¼ tsp white wine vinegar

To garnish:

shredded chilli

Chicken-wrapped asparagus
蠔油蘆筍雞卷

Use chicken breast instead of chicken thigh to wrap the asparagus because you need to be able to cut the meat into very thin slices. This is easier when you are using a very sharp knife, but be careful! This dish is the perfect accompaniment for noodles.

Peel the asparagus before cutting them into 2 cm lengths. Bring a pan of water to the boil and drop the asparagus in for about 30 seconds. Remove from the boiling water and refresh straight away.

Lay out the chicken slices. Dab a little cornflour on to each of the pieces to help the asparagus adhere to the chicken.

Place one length of asparagus on to one end of the chicken breast and roll it up, making sure there's only one layer of the chicken. Trim off any excess. Repeat the process for all 12 pieces of chicken.

Coat the wrapped parcels with cornflour and press it in with the palm of your hand.

Combine the eggs with 4 tbsp water in a bowl.

Coat the asparagus in the egg mixture, remove the excess and deep-fry at high heat until golden. This should take 3 minutes or so.

Meanwhile, mix all of the sauce ingredients except for the white wine vinegar together in a bowl and adjust the seasoning.

Heat the sauce in a pan before adding the chicken-wrapped asparagus and cooking for 2 minutes on medium heat.

Remove the sauce from the heat and add the white wine vinegar. Make sure it's stirred through the sauce thoroughly, and serve.

Makes 4 portions

4 asparagus spears

12 paper-thin slices of chicken breast

cornflour to dust

2 eggs, beaten

4 tbsp water

For the sauce:

4 tsp oyster sauce

2 tsp light soy sauce

4 tbsp water

2 tsp sugar

2 tsp Shaoxing wine

5 cm ginger, finely shredded

2 spring onions, finely shredded

2 chillies, finely shredded

2 tsp white wine vinegar

Chicken with red fermented bean curd

紅腐乳煸雞

You can serve any greens with this dish, not just pak choi. The flavours of the red fermented bean curd can be overpowering, so the greens will help to tone it down.

Mix the marinade ingredients together in a bowl. Taste and adjust the seasoning.

Add the chicken slices and leave to marinate for about 20 minutes.

Remove the chicken from the marinade (reserve the marinade) and coat with cornflour.

Heat a little oil in a wok until almost smoking.

Add the chicken to the wok and shallow-fry on a medium heat until the chicken begins to brown. This will take about 5 minutes. Remove the oil from the pan by tipping it into another pan or bowl for discarding later, and continue cooking both sides of the chicken until crispy.

Make a sauce with the reserved marinade by gently heating through in a small separate pan and reducing by a third. Once the sauce has reduced, add the Shaoxing wine just before serving.

To serve, arrange the pak choi on serving plates. Place the chicken on top of the pak choi. Drizzle the sauce over the chicken and garnish with deep-fried shallots.

Makes 4 portions

1 chicken breast, cut into wide thin slices

cornflour, to coat

oil, for frying

For the marinade:

2 water chestnuts, crushed

1 tbsp preserved red bean curd paste

4 tbsp garlic juice

salt and sugar, to taste

To serve:

2 tsp Shaoxing wine

pak choi leaves, blanched and refreshed

To garnish:

deep-fried shallots

Chicken and spinach fritters
鍋塔菠菜雞

You can use meat from the chicken breast or chicken thighs but the dish works best if you use a mix of the two. The fritters are cooked separately first before being finished off in the sauce so that they have a chance to set before taking on the flavours of the cooking sauce.

Blanch the spinach leaves in a pan of boiling water before refreshing and chopping finely.

Mix the minced chicken with the spinach, cashew nuts, water chestnuts, cornflour, salt and sugar in a bowl before forming into flattened balls.

Coat the chicken and spinach parcels with cornflour, then egg, before cooking.

Heat a little oil in a pan. Shallow-fry the chicken and spinach fritters. When the edges begin to take on colour, turn the parcels over to cook the other side.

Meanwhile, make a sauce by heating up all the sauce ingredients except for the white wine vinegar and the cornflour in a small pan. Taste and adjust the seasoning.

When the chicken and spinach fritters are ready, cook them in the sauce for about three minutes.

Add the vinegar and slaked cornflour. Cook to thicken before serving.

Makes 4 portions

100g spinach leaves

200g chicken mince

1 tbsp cooked cashew nuts, finely chopped

3 water chestnuts, finely chopped

1 tbsp cornflour

½ tsp salt

½ tsp sugar

cornflour to coat

beaten egg to coat

For the sauce:

1 cm ginger, shredded

½ fresh red chilli, shredded

½ spring onion, shredded

1½ tbsp water

½ tsp salt

1 tsp light soy sauce

1tsp Shaoxing wine

salt and sugar to taste

½ tsp white wine vinegar

1 tsp slaked cornflour

Guinea fowl
and ginseng soup
蔘絲枸杞炖珠雞

Guinea fowl or chicken works best in this soup. The ginseng adds an intense aroma and imparts its restorative properties to the soup as it's said that ginseng can boost the immune system. But avoid gamey meats as they will clash with the ginseng.

Bring a pan of water to the boil and add the guinea fowl pieces. When the impurities rise to the surface, remove the guinea fowl with a slotted spoon and rinse in cool water.

Place the guinea fowl and the rest of the ingredients in a flameproof casserole and cover with water. Put the lid on the casserole dish. Either slow-cook on the hob on a low heat for 2 hours or in a preheated oven at 150°C/gas mark 3 for 2 hours.

Makes 8 portions

1 whole guinea fowl skin on, split into 8 pieces (ask your butcher to do this for you)

50g goji berries

100g whole ginseng roots

5 cm piece fresh ginger, sliced

2 spring onion stalks

1 tsp salt

Steamed duck with lotus root and *dong gua* sauce
冬瓜鴨肉扣

This dish is filled with traditional Taiwanese flavours. The *dong gua* sauce for example, is salted winter gourd that's been preserved with liquorice and sour plums to give its unique flavour. It's very popular as an ingredient in Taiwan but can be quite hard to find here. If you can't find dong gua, look for dong cai, salted greengage or salted prune.

Bring a small pan of water to the boil with a teaspoon of salt and the ginger. Add the duck and reduce the heat down to a simmer. Cook the duck for about 20 minutes before removing and cooling.

When the duck is cold, cut into thin slices.

Set your steamer on top of a pan of boiling water. On a plate, arrange the finely sliced lotus root at the bottom and the sliced duck breast on top. The amount of each you will need depends on the size of your plate but should be around three slices of each per portion. Steam for 5 minutes.

Meanwhile, make the dressing by warming all the ingredients in a small pan until heated through.

When the duck is ready, drizzle the dressing over the top. Top with the *dong gua* sauce and garnish with ginger, chilli and spring onions.

Makes 4 portions

1 duck breast, skin on

1 length lotus root, peeled and thinly sliced

2½ cm ginger, sliced

For the dressing:

1 tbsp stock

1 tsp Shaoxing wine

½ tsp white wine vinegar

salt and sugar to taste

To serve:

1 tsp *dong gua* sauce

To garnish:

chilli, spring onion and ginger

Duck and lotus root parcels
腐乳蓮香鴨

The lotus root adds a lovely crunch to this dish which makes a great contrast in texture from the duck breast. You can also serve the sauce on the side as a dip.

Cut the lotus root slices in half so they're a similar size to the duck slices.

Make the filling by mixing the chicken mince with the red preserved bean curd, smashed water chestnuts and the spring onions together in a bowl.

Sandwich the filling between a slice of duck breast and a slice of lotus root.

Bring a good amount of oil to nearly smoking in a wok.

Coat the exposed filling with cornflour. If you're having trouble making the flour stick, use a little water. Coat the whole parcel with a little beaten egg before frying until golden.

When the parcels turn golden, heat a frying pan on the hob without any oil in it and crisp up the sides of the parcels in the pan.

Make the sauce by heating through the red preserved bean curd, garlic juice, black pepper, basil leaves and stock in a separate pan.

As the sauce reduces, add the slaked cornflour to thicken the sauce and then add the shallot oil. Season to taste.

When the duck parcels are ready, cut in half and drizzle with sauce to serve.

Makes 6 portions

1 lotus root, peeled and sliced

1 duck breast, skin on, cut into thin slices

cornflour to coat

beaten egg to coat

For the filling:

250g chicken mince

6 tbsp red preserved bean curd

6 water chestnuts, smashed

3 spring onions, cut into medallions

For the sauce:

6 tsp red preserved bean curd

6 tsp garlic juice

½ tsp ground black pepper

15 sweet basil leaves, finely chopped

6 tsp shallot oil

180ml stock

3 tsp slaked cornflour

salt and sugar to taste

Pork
豬肉

Pork with chilli sauce
椒鹽里肌

Marinating the meat before cooking tenderises it and allows it to absorb flavours more easily. Remember to dress the meat at the last minute so that it's still crispy when you eat it.

Cut the pork into strips and place in a bowl. Pour the garlic juice, Shaoxing wine, white wine vinegar and Chinese five spice over the pork and leave to marinate for about 10 minutes.

Remove the pork pieces from the marinade and coat them with cornflour.

Heat a generous amount of oil in a wok, and deep-fry the pork until it's golden.

When the pork is cooked, remove it from the wok and discard most of the oil. Stir-fry the chilli, minced garlic and spring onion in the wok for a minute or so. Add the pork back to the wok and season with salt and Sichuan peppercorns.

Stir-fry for a further minute before removing from the heat. Transfer the pork to serving plates and serve with a drizzle of Sichuan chilli sauce.

Makes 4 portions

1 pork chop

50ml garlic juice
(See page 30)

1 tsp Shaoxing wine

1 tsp white wine vinegar

½ tsp Chinese five spice

1 tbsp cornflour, to coat

1 red chilli, finely sliced

1 garlic clove, minced

1 spring onion, cut into medallions

salt and crushed Sichuan peppercorns, to taste

To serve:

½ tbsp Sichuan chilli sauce
(see recipe on page 252)

Salted pork
客家鹹肉

Salted pork is a Hakka-style dish that originated from the tradition of praying to spirits. For each spirit prayed to, a new piece of meat had to be offered in appeasement. As a result, families ended up with more meat than they could eat. Curing the meat with salt meant it could be stored and eaten in the coming months. The curing of the meat is a long and slow process and this recipe requires the pork to be marinated overnight.

Cut the pork belly into 5 cm-wide lengths.

For the rub, mix the peppercorns, salt and garlic together in a bowl, then add the sesame oil and mix well. Rub the mixture into the pork so that the pork is coated all over. Allow the meat to rest in the rub overnight.

The next day, heat a griddle pan and cook the sides of the pork only (not the skin or the meat) on a medium heat without adding oil.

When the sides are crispy, the pork should be cooked through.

Mix all the ingredients for the dressing together in a bowl and adjust seasoning to taste.

When the meat is ready, cut the pork into thin slices. Allow 2 or 3 slices per portion and serve on top of a bed of shredded lettuce and drizzle with the dressing.

Makes 4 portions

200g belly pork

For the rub:

¼ tbsp crushed Sichuan peppercorns

½ tbsp salt

1 garlic clove, crushed

¼ tsp sesame oil

For the dressing:

1 garlic clove, finely sliced

½ tbsp white wine vinegar

pinch of sugar

To serve:

shredded lettuce

Noodles stir-fried with pork and bean sprouts
肉絲芽菜燜麵

This versatile noodle stir-fry also works with chicken, beef, lamb and seafood. Use the fresh noodles you find in the chiller cabinet in the supermarket as these give a bit more bite without drying out during the cooking process.

In a bowl, mix all of the ingredients for the sauce and adjust the seasoning.

Heat a little oil in a wok until smoking and stir-fry the pork until the meat begins to brown.

Add the sauce and 2 tablespoons of cooking oil to the wok and stir through.

When the sauce has reduced a little, add the cooked noodles and bean sprouts to warm through.

Add the Chinese chives at the last minute before serving.

Makes 4 portions

100g pork fillet, finely sliced

2 x 300g pack fresh cooked noodles

100g bean sprouts

handful yellow Chinese garlic chives

vegetable oil, for frying

For the sauce:

2 spring onions, thinly sliced on the diagonal

100ml chicken stock

5 cm piece fresh ginger

2 tbsp light soy sauce

1 tsp ground white pepper

1 tsp salt

Slow cooked pork with *Mei Cai*
梅菜封肉

This is a traditional Hakka-style dish. *Mei cai* is a variety of pickled mustard greens from the Guangdong province in China and in this recipe we use the dried version, which usually comes in a jar or earthenware pot. The meat must be cooked to the point of falling apart to really achieve the right texture. The fat from the belly will keep the lean meat moist. Deep-fry the pork belly first so the skin crisps up. This will help the meat cook and really soak in the flavours from the mei cai sauce.

Depending on the size of your pork belly, you will need to cut it into portions about 5 cm in width.

Bring a pan of water to the boil, make sure it's enough to cover the pork belly.

Cook the pork belly in boiling water briefly until the meat changes colour, approximately 2 minutes. This removes the blood and any impurities.

Remove the meat from the pan and place into a bowl and rub dark soy sauce into it.

Heat a good glug of oil in a wok and deep-fry the meat on medium heat. You must put the skin side in first. When it's ready, it will be golden and crispy on the outside. It will take about 4-5 minutes.

Meanwhile, soak the mei cai in warm water to allow it to open. Wash it before using to remove the sand.

Finely chop the mei cai before stir-frying it in a separate wok with ginger, garlic, spring onion and soy sauce. Cook for about 2 minutes until the vegetables become aromatic.

In a bowl, mix together the ingredients for the mei cai sauce together with the cooked mei cai. Adjust the seasoning.

Makes 6 portions

250g pork belly

dark soy sauce for the rub

200g mei cai

1 cm ginger, shredded

1 garlic clove, minced

½ spring onion, cut into medallions

½ tbsp light soy sauce

For the mei cai sauce:

15g palm sugar

½ tbsp dark soy sauce

1 orange peel, chopped

1 cm ginger, sliced

1 whole garlic clove, skin on

½ spring onion, cut into three

1 tsp Shaoxing wine

½ fresh red chilli, finely chopped

Set your bamboo steamer over a pan of simmering water. Cut the pork belly into slices ½ cm thick. Line the slices up on a tray, skin side down. Pour the mei cai sauce evenly over the top and steam for two hours.

After the meat is cooked through, garnish with spring onions before serving. Allow three slices per portion.

To garnish:

1 spring onion, cut into medallions

Little Lion's Head with tofu
迷你獅子頭

This is an alternative to the original Little Lion's Head, using an oyster sauce rather than a light dressing. The method is a bit different too. The addition of the oyster sauce will also make this dish a lot more savoury.

Mix the seasoning for the meatballs together first and adjust to taste before adding to the minced pork, water chestnuts and reconstituted mushrooms.

Form the mince mixture into balls and lightly coat with cornflour.

Deep-fry until golden before removing from the heat and set aside.

Make the sauce by mixing all of the sauce ingredients except for the white wine vinegar together in a bowl and adjusting the seasoning. Add to the pan with the tofu and gently heat through.

When the tofu is heated through, about 2 minutes, remove from the sauce.

Add the slaked cornflour to the sauce and cook through to thicken it. Stir through the white wine vinegar at the last minute.

Serve with the poached mustard greens at the bottom, then the tofu squares and finally the meatballs with a drizzle of the sauce on top. Sprinkle over a little chopped spring onion and chilli, and serve.

Makes 4 portions

150g pork belly, minced

2 water chestnuts, minced

2 dried Chinese mushrooms, reconstituted and finely chopped

2 tsp cornflour

tofu as required

For the meatball seasoning:

1 tsp salt

1 tsp sugar

1½ tsp white pepper

2 garlic cloves, minced

2 tsp dried shrimp

2 tsp chopped spring onion

For the sauce:

2 tsp oyster sauce

6 tbsp chicken stock

1 tsp soy sauce

1 tsp Shaoxing wine

½ tsp salt

1 tsp sugar

2 tsp slaked cornflour

1 tsp white wine vinegar

To serve:

poached mustard greens

1 spring onion, roughly chopped

½ fresh red chilli, finely chopped

Pork mince and aubergine stir-fry
肉末茄子

The key to this dish is in the cooking of the aubergine. Make sure the aubergine has softened before adding the sauce. If you need to increase the cooking time, add more water to the wok.

Mix all the sauce ingredients together in a bowl and adjust seasoning to taste.

Heat a little oil in a wok until almost smoking. Add the pork mince and cook until it changes colour.

Add the aubergine with about 10 tbsp water and cook for about 3–4 minutes until the aubergine has softened.

Add the sauce to the pan and stir through before adding the slaked cornflour, white wine vinegar and sesame oil. When the sauce has thickened, it's ready to serve.

Makes 4 portions

1 tbsp pork mince

1 aubergine, cut into 5 cm batons

about 10 tbsp water

1 tsp slaked cornflour

1 tsp white wine vinegar

½ tsp sesame oil

oil, for frying

For the sauce:

3 tbsp chicken stock

1 tsp miso paste

2 garlic cloves, finely chopped

¼ fresh red chilli, cut into fine slivers

10 coriander stalks, finely chopped

salt and sugar, to taste

Bamboo cup soup
竹節盅湯

This deliciously aromatic soup is steamed and served in a bamboo cup. It was originally made with pigeon but using pork means that you can make it year round. Chicken is a good alternative. The bamboo cup adds to the flavours of the soup, making it fresher, lighter and more herbaceous. If you can't get hold of bamboo cups, you can also use normal cups, as long as they're suitable for steaming.

Poach the Chinese mushrooms in hot stock for 10 minutes, until reconstituted. Remove from the stock and finely chop. Set aside and allow to cool.

Meanwhile, mix all of the ingredients in a bowl for the broth and taste to adjust seasoning.

Mix the pork mince, mushrooms, water chestnuts and broth together until combined. You need quite a runny but thick mixture. Add more stock if needed.

Allow the mixture to rest for an hour.

Stir the soup mixture again before adding it to the bamboo cups.

Steam the soup for 30 minutes. After steaming, top with spring onion, ginger and deep-fried shallots and serve.

Makes 4 portions

160g minced pork

10 dried Chinese mushrooms

10 water chestnuts, minced

stock to cover the mushrooms

For the broth:

400 ml chicken stock

2 tbsp Shaoxing wine

2 tsp salt

2 tsp sugar

1 tsp ground white pepper

2 tbsp shallot oil

2 tbsp soy sauce

To garnish:

chopped spring onion, shredded ginger and deep-fried shallots

Egg-wrapped soup
花開富貴

This dish is beautiful to look at; the way the crêpe opens up is like a flower, especially when you add the stock and the leaves float up like the petals in a water lily. It's really quite stunning and serene.

Start by making a thin crêpe with just the eggs. Put a little oil into a frying pan and heat until nearly smoking. Put a thin layer of the beaten egg into the bottom of your frying pan and fry until set.

Mix all of the seasoning together in a bowl and adjust for flavour.

In a bowl, mix the finely chopped mushroom with the ham hock.

Put the minced pork in the bowl with the seasoning.

Line a large bowl, around 20 cm in diameter, with the crêpe. Place the crab meat in the centre at the bottom of the bowl on the crepe.

Arrange the quail's eggs in a circle around the crab meat, white side down.

Arrange the ham hock mix to the outer edges of the quail's eggs, without covering the eggs.

Put the seasoned minced pork on top of the crab meat, quail's eggs and ham hock in one uniform layer.

In the centre, you should have a void. Put the mooli balls into the centre and press down so that it's even.

If there's excess crêpe left, fold over the middle.

In the middle, add a pinch of salt, the ginger and spring onion.

Cover loosely with cling film and steam for 20 minutes.

Leave the parcel to rest for 30 minutes and then turn the pork mince parcel into a bigger bowl. You should now have an upturned dome.

Makes 8 portions

2 eggs, beaten

6 quail's eggs, hard boiled and halved

400g minced pork

3 water chestnuts, finely chopped

80g shredded meat from ham hock

6 dried Chinese mushrooms, reconstituted and finely chopped

12 mooli balls, made with melon baller

2 tbsp minced crab meat

1 slice ginger

1 spring onion stalk

pinch of salt

stock to cover

For the seasoning:

1 tsp ground white pepper

1 tsp sesame oil

1 tsp Shaoxing wine

pinch salt

½ tbsp cornflour

Carefully cut the crêpe into eight equal portions, as you might divide a cake, without cutting through the whole parcel, and pull back the crêpe to reveal a flower.

Add warmed stock to the bowl until the crêpe leaves begin to float like a flower.

Garnish with the cherry tomato in the middle and serve.

To serve:

½ cherry tomato

Stuffed pig's trotters with pak choi
紅燒豬蹄

This recipe is quite time-consuming, but believe me, the dish is simply delicious. It's well worth the effort despite the time it takes to cook. Cooking the trotters in boiling water briefly before stewing helps to remove the blood and impurities in them and therefore improves the taste. The trotters can be eaten hot or cold but be careful to adjust the cooking time accordingly to ensure the stuffing is cooked through.

Bring a large pan of water to the boil.

Before cooking the pig's trotters, scrape off any hairs with a knife. For any fine hairs, you can singe them off. Rinse the trotters in cold water.

Add the trotters to the boiling water and cook for about 2-3 minutes until the flesh changes colour. Remove to a plate and set aside. Discard the water from the pan.

Again boil enough water to cover the trotters and add all of the ingredients for the stewing liquor to the pan. Try the mixture before adding the trotters to make sure you have the right balance of saltiness and sweetness.

Simmer the pig's trotters on a low heat for 30 minutes with the lid on.

After half an hour, remove the trotters and lay them down on a tray separately. Set aside and reserve the cooking liquor.

When the trotters are cool enough to handle, remove the bones. You should have 16 roughly equal portions.

—› *See over*

Makes 8 portions

To stew the pig's trotters:

4 pig's trotters, cut into four equal portions (your butcher will be able to do this for you)

For the stewing liquid:

2 star anise

1 cinnamon stick

2 cm ginger, sliced

2 whole garlic cloves, skin on

1 orange peel

1 tsp Sichuan peppercorns

1 spring onion, cut into three

1 tbsp dark soy sauce

1 tbsp Shaoxing wine

½ tbsp Chinese black vinegar

1 tsp salt

30g palm sugar

1 whole fresh red chilli

5 slices of dried liquorice

water to cover

Mix all of the ingredients for the filling together in a bowl.

Dust the trotter portions with cornflour on the inside before adding the filling. You need about a teaspoon of filling for each portion, depending on the size of the trotter. It will be easier to stuff the trotter if you form the filling into quenelles. The cornflour will help it stick.

Wrap the trotter parcels tightly in cling film.

Reboil the cooking liquor, turn off the heat and add the trotter parcels. Allow the trotters to cook in the residual heat with the lid on until the liquor is cool.

When the cooking liquor is cold (3-4 hours) the trotters are ready for the final dish.

Put your steamer over a pan of boiling water.

Carefully remove the cling film from the trotter parcel and steam on a plate for about 5 minutes until warmed through.

Meanwhile, blanch and refresh the pak choi.

Mix all of the ingredients for the dressing in a bowl and adjust the seasoning.

When the trotter parcel has been warmed through, place each parcel on top of a leaf of the pak choi and drizzle with a teaspoon of the dressing. Allow 2 leaves and parcels per portion, garnish with finely shredded red chilli and serve.

To make the stuffed pig's trotters:

cornflour to coat

For the filling:

100g minced pork

3 water chestnuts, chopped

30g dried Chinese mushroom, reconstituted and finely chopped

½ tbsp cornflour

To make the final dish:

16 leaves pak choi

For the dressing:

8 tsp soy sauce

8 tsp black vinegar

8 tsp shallot oil

red chilli to garnish

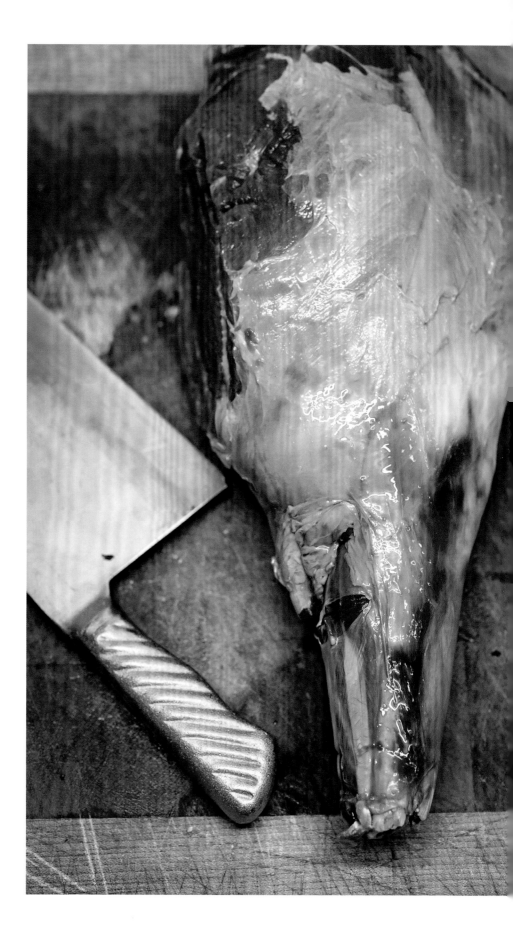

Lamb
羊肉

Lamb with hot spicy sauce
滷水羔羊

Stewing the lamb first helps to keep the meat moist when you deep-fry it. All the flavours of the lamb are also absorbed into the meat during the cooking process. Without the stewing, the meat would be much drier.

Put all of the ingredients for the stewing liquor in a pan. Taste and adjust seasoning.

Bring the liquid to the boil before adding the ribs. Once the ribs have been added, turn the heat down to a simmer and slow cook them for 30 minutes or until the sauce is reduced. The meat should be just about to fall off the bone.

Turn the heat off the pan and let the ribs cool in the cooking liquor.

Once the lamb has cooled, cut the ribs into bite-size portions and coat with cornflour. Be sure to press the cornflour in with your hand.

Heat a generous amount of oil in a wok until almost smoking and deep-fry the lamb on high heat until the edges crisp up and begin to turn golden.

Meanwhile, make the dressing by mixing all of the sauce ingredients in a bowl and adjust for seasoning.

When the lamb is ready, take it out of the wok and put it on a plate. Drizzle over the dressing and garnish with the spring onion and chilli.

Makes 4 portions

100g lamb ribs

cornflour to coat

For the stewing liquor:

3 star anise

1 cinnamon stick

8 slices of dried liquorice

1½ tsp Chinese five spice

5 cm ginger, sliced

3 whole garlic cloves

2 spring onions, cut into three

2 tbsp Shaoxing wine

pinch of sugar

water to cover

For the dressing:

1 tsp minced garlic

1 spring onion, cut into medallions

2 tbsp Sichuan chilli sauce

salt and Sichuan peppercorn to taste

½ tsp sugar

1 tsp white wine vinegar

1 tbsp water

½ tsp sesame oil

To garnish:

spring onion, chopped
fresh red chilli, shredded

Lamb and celery stir-fry
香芹炒羊腿肉

For the accompanying vegetables in this dish, you can use spring onion, mangetout and other crunchy greens. Celery is best because it balances the heat from the lamb.

Mix all the sauce ingredients together in a bowl and adjust seasoning to taste. Set aside.

Heat a little oil in a wok until nearly smoking. Coat the lamb in cornflour and stir-fry in the hot oil. Once the lamb is coated in oil, add the celery.

When the meat changes colour, add the sauce and stir-fry for a further minute.

Just before removing from the heat, add the red wine vinegar and the sesame oil. Warm through and serve.

Makes 4 portions

100g lamb leg steak, thinly sliced

cornflour, to coat

2 celery sticks, cut into 2½ cm lengths

oil, for frying

For the sauce:

10 sweet basil leaves, whole

2½ cm piece fresh ginger, thinly sliced

4 dried chillies

2 tsp soy sauce

2 tsp shallot oil

salt and sugar, to taste

To serve:

1 tsp red wine vinegar

2 tsp sesame oil

Red roast lamb stew
微火嫩燒羊腩

This is a classic Chinese dish which you can make with lamb, pork or beef. You can use stock or water here but stock gives greater flavour. For the garlic, I leave the clove whole and the skin on so you can remove it at a later stage, if you wish. If you take the skin off, the garlic will disintegrate during the cooking process.

Cut the lamb belly into large bite-size chunks.

Cook the lamb in boiling water for about five minutes until the meat changes colour and remove from the water.

In a pan, add all the sauce ingredients except the lamb and the tofu stick and bring to the boil. Taste and adjust for seasoning before adding the lamb.

Turn the heat down to a gentle simmer and cook with the lid on.

After about an hour's cooking time, add the tofu stick and cook for a further 30 minutes.

Once the meat and tofu stick have both softened, pass the cooking juices through a colander.

In a pan, reduce the sauce and thicken with slaked cornflour. Season to taste.

When serving, drizzle the thickened sauce over a mix of the meat and tofu stick.

Makes 4 portions

500g lamb belly

50g dried tofu stick

For the sauce:

50ml soy sauce

1 cinnamon stick

2 star anise

2 lengths dried orange peel

1 fresh red chilli

2 tbsp Chinese black vinegar

1 tbsp Shaoxin wine

½ tbsp palm sugar

2½ cm ginger, sliced

2 whole garlic cloves, skin on

1 spring onion stalk

stock or water to coat

1 tsp slaked cornflour

Lamb with garlic stem and wood ear mushrooms
蒜苔木耳炒羊

Even though there's nothing crispy in this dish, it's best eaten as soon as it's cooked. The meat will harden as it cools, and reheating it would result in overcooked meat.

Mix all of the ingredients for the marinade together in a bowl and adjust for seasoning. Add the lamb to the bowl and leave to marinate for 15 minutes.

Meanwhile, mix all of the ingredients for the sauce together in a separate bowl, and adjust the seasoning.

Remove the marinated lamb from the marinade and dust with cornflour.

Heat a little oil in a wok, until nearly smoking.

Shallow-fry the meat briefly in the wok until it changes colour, then remove to a plate.

Add the sauce, the garlic stem, mushroom, ginger, spring onion, coriander leaves and red chilli to the wok and stir through briefly until it becomes aromatic.

Return the lamb to the wok and stir through before serving. Garnish with slices of red chilli.

Makes 4 portions

100g lamb leg steak, cut into strips

1 tbsp cornflour, to coat

30g garlic stem, cut into 2½ cm lengths

10g wood ear mushroom, thinly sliced

2½ cm piece fresh ginger, thinly sliced

½ spring onion, thinly sliced

a few coriander leaves

½ fresh red chilli, finely sliced

For the marinade:

½ tsp salt

1 tsp soy sauce

½ tsp ground white pepper

For the sauce:

1 tsp Shaoxing wine

¼ tsp salt

¼ tsp sugar

1 tsp white wine vinegar

2 tbsp chicken stock

1 tsp slaked cornflour

½ tsp sesame oil

1 tsp soy sauce

To garnish:

sliced red chillies

Angelica root lamb stew
當歸燉羊盅

The delicate broth of this angelica root lamb stew is surprisingly warming. It's perfect for a cold winter's day as a healthy, hearty stew. For a more filling dish, add some super-thin noodles towards the end.

Preheat the oven to 150°C/gas mark 2.

Bring a pan of water to the boil and cook the lamb briefly until the meat changes colour.

Remove the lamb to a casserole dish and add the rest of the ingredients.

Cook the casserole in the oven for around 2 hours. You may need to top it up with more stock.

When the lamb is tender and cooked, stir in a few drops of rose liqueur before serving.

Makes 4 portions

300g lamb leg steak, cut into bite-size chunks

5 slices dried angelica root

1 tbsp goji berries

½ tsp salt

½ tsp sugar

2 tbsp rice wine

5 cm piece fresh ginger, smashed

1 spring onion stalk

1 litre chicken stock, plus more if needed

To serve:

a few drops of rose liqueur

Beef
牛肉

Beef with Chinese water spinach
空心菜炒牛肉

The fermented bean curd sauce has a tendency to burn so even though this is a stir-fry dish, you need to cook it on medium heat. That's why the beef and the Chinese water spinach are cooked separately first, before the sauce is added.

Coat the beef ribeye with the cornflour and beaten egg before shallow-frying in a wok. Once the meat changes colour, remove from the heat and set aside.

Mix all of the ingredients for the sauce together in a bowl and mix into a paste. Add the water to the paste to dilute it into a sauce, adding more if necessary. Adjust seasoning.

In a wok, stir-fry the water spinach briefly before returning the beef to the heat.

As the water spinach begins to wilt, add all the ingredients for the sauce except the sesame oil and red wine vinegar and warm through.

Add the red wine vinegar and sesame oil just before removing from the heat. Adjust for seasoning and serve.

Makes 4 portions

100g beef rib-eye, cut into slices

1 egg, beaten

cornflour to coat

50g Chinese water spinach

For the sauce:

2½ cm shredded ginger

2 tsp fermented bean curd

1 tsp malt vinegar

2 tbsp stock

2 tsp Shaoxing wine

large pinch crushed Sichuan peppercorns

sugar to taste

4 tbsp water

½ tsp red wine vinegar

1 tsp sesame oil

Beef and orange peel stir-fry
陳皮溜牛肉

You must use dried orange peel to impart the best flavour to the meat in this dish. Fresh orange peel doesn't taste as good and doesn't have the same sort of savoury notes. You can also add sweet basil and coriander just before serving for a slight variation in the flavour.

Soak the orange peel in a bowl of hot water until it softens. Scrape away any remaining pith so it's only the peel left before finely slicing into strands.

Poach the orange peel in stock for about 5 minutes. Remove the orange peel from the stock and set both aside.

Mix the stock in a bowl with the ginger, salt, sugar, and vinegar to taste.

Meanwhile, coat the slivers of beef with the cornflour.

Heat a small amount of oil in a wok until nearly smoking and quickly stir-fry the beef.

When the beef changes colour, add the orange peel and the seasoned stock.

Cook for a minute longer and add the red wine vinegar right at the last minute before removing from the pan. Garnish with finely sliced spring onion.

Makes 4 portions

2 dried orange peels

50ml stock

2½ cm finely sliced ginger

salt and sugar to taste

1 tsp red wine vinegar

100g beef rib-eye, cut into fine slivers

cornflour to coat

To garnish:

5 spring onion stalks, finely sliced

Beef with sweet basil
九層塔炒牛肉

The meat in this dish needs to cook through very quickly in order to stay tender, though the herbs will wilt during cooking. For the best flavours, you should eat it straight away.

Mix all of the sauce ingredients together in a bowl. Taste and adjust seasoning.

Heat a little oil in a wok until almost smoking. Coat the beef with the cornflour and then the beaten egg and stir-fry briefly in the oil until it changes colour.

Add the sauce and continue to cook quickly for about 1 minute before adding the ginger, spring onions, chilli and basil leaves to the pan. Stir through before serving.

Makes 4 portions

200g beef rib-eye,
cut into strips

1 egg, beaten

1 tbsp cornflour

2½ cm piece fresh ginger,
cut into slices

2 spring onions, cut into medallions

1 red chilli, sliced

10 sweet basil leaves

oil, for frying

For the sauce:

1 tsp light soy sauce

1 tsp Shaoxing wine

½ tsp sesame oil

1 tbsp stock

½ tsp red wine vinegar

1 tsp slaked cornflour

salt and sugar, to taste

Red oil beef
紅油嫩牛

The beef in this dish is served medium rare so make sure your meat is good quality. The meat needs to be cut very thinly so that the heat from the hot oil is enough to cook it.

In a bowl, mix all of the sauce ingredients together. Adjust seasoning. You need a sauce that's hot and numbing.

Heat the sauce in a wok on a medium heat for about 1 minute until it becomes hot and fragrant.

Add the beef and quickly stir through before removing from the heat. Ideally, the beef should be medium rare but you can cook it for longer if desired.

Garnish with ginger and coriander, and serve straight away.

Makes 4 portions

150g rib-eye beef, cut into thin strips about 1 cm in width

For the sauce:

1 tbsp red chilli sauce

2½ cm piece fresh ginger, finely shredded

1 tsp tian mian jiang

2 spring onions, cut into medallions

2 tsp crushed Sichuan peppercorns

1 tsp red wine vinegar

2 tbsp water

1 tsp sesame oil

1 tsp chilli oil

salt and sugar, to taste

To garnish:

finely shredded ginger

coriander leaves

Beef and mushroom stir-fry
醬爆牛肉

The beef in this dish stays tender because it's cooked very quickly.
You can serve other greens with this but celery is by far the best as its
crunchy bite offers a contrast to the texture of the meat.

Poach the shiitake mushrooms in hot stock until they plump up again. Remove from the stock and cut the mushrooms into thin slices.

Bring a pan of water to the boil and poach the celery until just tender usually about 3 minutes.

Mix all the sauce ingredients together in a bowl and adjust seasoning.

Coat the beef in the cornflour and then a little beaten egg.

Heat a little oil in a wok until nearly smoking, then add the beef and stir-fry briefly, until the beef changes colour.

Add the sauce and the mushrooms to the wok and stir-fry for another minute to warm through before serving.

Arrange the poached celery on serving plates and place the cooked beef and mushrooms on top. Drizzle the sauce over them, then serve garnished with shredded chilli and spring onion.

Makes 6 portions

2 dried shiitake mushrooms

100ml stock, for soaking the mushrooms

100g rib-eye beef, tenderised and cut into slivers

1 egg, beaten

cornflour

oil, for frying

For the sauce:

1 tsp red and green chillies, thinly sliced

1 spring onion, thinly sliced

2 garlic cloves, thinly sliced

1 tbsp tian mian jiang

½ tsp Sichuan chilli sauce (see recipe on page 252)

1 tsp light soy sauce

1 tsp Shaoxing wine

½ tsp golden syrup

½ tbsp water

¼ tsp red wine vinegar

¼ tsp sesame oil

1 tsp slaked cornflour

To serve:

1 celery stick, cut into 2½ cm chunks

To garnish:

shredded chilli and spring onion

Beef fried rice
牛肉炒飯

Prawn or chicken would make good alternatives to beef in this dish but they must be cooked through before they are added to the rice. Fresh lotus root is best for this recipe because it retains its crunch.

Heat the oil in a wok over a low heat. Add the garlic and stir-fry for about 1 minute until it becomes slightly softer.

Remove the pan from the heat, then add the beaten egg and stir through until it's scrambled.

Return the pan to the heat and cook the egg until it begins to brown and you can begin to smell the garlic.

Stir in the cooked rice and when it starts to crisp and pop, add the rest of the ingredients except for the beef.

When the rice starts to change colour, add the beef and stir through.

When the beef has browned slightly, it's ready to serve.

Makes 6 portions

1 tbsp oil, for frying

1 garlic clove, minced

½ egg, beaten

500g cooked rice

1 tbsp tomato ketchup

½ spring onion, finely chopped

1 tbsp chopped lotus root

pinch of salt

pinch of ground white pepper

20g rib-eye beef, thinly sliced

❛ Use fresh lotus root so that it retains its crunch ❜

Offal
內臟

Tripe in spicy sauce
滷水辣牛肚

The carrot and the mooli in the stewing mix add a depth of flavour to the tripe, but you can leave out either if you want. The tripe dries out easily so be sure to work as quickly as possible. For this reason, it's just not possible to make a smaller quantity of this dish. Adding the Sichuan peppercorns at the last minute will help to keep the fragrant peppery notes fresh.

First, add all the ingredients for the cooking liquor to a large pan and bring to the boil. When the water is boiling, taste and adjust for seasoning.

Add the tripe and gently simmer for 1 hour with the lid on. Make sure the tripe is covered with the cooking liquor at all times, and add more water if necessary.

After 1 hour, remove the tripe and allow to cool but do not let it dry out. Reserve the cooking liquor.

When the tripe is cold, cut into bite-size slices about 5 cm wide. To do this, cut diagonally through the tripe to achieve a slice that's thicker at one end and thinner at the other. You'll need around three or four slices per serving.

Meanwhile, make the dressing by mixing all of the ingredients, except the Sichuan peppercorns, together in a bowl. Taste and adjust seasoning.

Mix the tripe with the dressing, then add the Sichuan peppercorns and mix thoroughly.

Divide the tripe into separate portions.

Place each portion of tripe on top of shredded lettuce and drizzle with any remaining dressing. Garnish with coriander and serve.

Makes 10 portions

500g cleaned tripe

For the cooking liquor:

3 star anise

1 cinnamon stick

peel from 1 orange

2½ cm ginger

2 garlic cloves

1 spring onion

1 fresh red chilli

1 tsp cumin

1 tsp tian mian jiang

1 tsp dark soy sauce

1 tsp red wine vinegar

30g palm sugar

1 litre water

1 carrot, cut into big chunks

1 mooli, cut into big chunks

For the dressing:

100ml cooking liquor (see left)

7.5 cm piece fresh ginger, finely chopped

8 garlic cloves, minced

10 tsp Sichuan chilli sauce (see recipe on page 252)

10 tsp red wine vinegar

10 tsp chilli oil

10 tsp shallot oil

5 tsp sugar

5 tsp crushed Sichuan peppercorns

To serve:

shredded lettuce

To garnish:

coriander, to garnish

Ox tongue with marmalade
大吉大利

Da ji da li (大吉大利) is the Chinese name for this dish. The name is very auspicious as ji li means luck in Chinese while da means big. But the character for ji also sounds like orange while the character for li sounds like tongue. So naturally a dish of orange and tongue is very lucky but it also sounds great.

Place the ox tongue in a pan of simmering water for about 3-4 minutes, until a white film forms on the outside. When the film forms, remove the tongue from the water and scrape the film off.

Meanwhile, in a pan, add all of the ingredients for the stewing liquor and bring to the boil. Taste and adjust seasoning.

After the ox tongue is cleaned, simmer in the stewing liquid for 90 minutes.

Blanche the mangetout in stock for about 1 minute and refresh in cold water.

When you're ready to serve, finely slice the ox tongue. You need about 4-5 slices per portion.

Make the sauce by mixing all of the ingredients together. Taste and adjust seasoning.

Serve the ox tongue on top of the mangetout and dress with the sauce. Garnish with ginger and deep-fried shallots and serve.

Makes 8 portions

1 ox tongue

For the stewing liquor:

1/2 tbsp red wine vinegar

1 tbsp Sichuan peppercorns

3 star anise

6 slices of dried liquorice

5 cm ginger, sliced

2 spring onion stalks

1 fresh red chilli

2 whole garlic cloves

2 tbsp Shaoxing wine

1 cinnamon stick

½ tbsp salt

water to cover

20g palm sugar

For the sauce:

1 tbsp marmalade

zest from half an orange

¼ tsp white wine vinegar

½ tsp sesame oil

½ tsp water

To garnish:

shredded fresh ginger
and deep-fried shallots

To serve:

5 mangetout

Pig's blood and intestines
五更腸旺

Wu geng chang wang (五更肠旺) is the name of this dish in Chinese. Chang wang stands for intestines while Wu geng is an indication of time, 5am to be precise, in old Chinese. The name originated from the tradition of farmers slaughtering their pigs at dawn before selling their wares at market. Left to the farmer for consumption is the offal, or blood and intestines in this case. While this dish uses ingredients you may not be used to, I urge you to try it – the yielding texture of the offal combined with the spicy Sichuan chili sauce is absolutely delicious.

Prepare the intestines by washing them inside out. Poach in boiling water until the colour changes before removing and allowing to cool.

Gently pan-fry the pig's blood until it gets a coating on the outside, being careful not to break it.

Mix all of the sauce ingredients in a bowl. Taste and adjust seasoning.

Heat the sauce gently in a wok. As the sauce begins to bubble, add the pig's blood, intestines, ginger and spring onions. Cook for about 3 minutes.

When the blood and intestines are heated through, add the shallot oil, stir through and serve.

Makes 4 portions

8 x 5 cm length pig's intestines

120g set pig's blood, cubed

3 spring onions, finely chopped

3 cm ginger, shredded

2 tsp shallot oil

For the sauce:

4 tbsp Sichuan chilli sauce

2 tsp tian mian jiang

1 tsp minced garlic

8 tbsp chicken stock

2 tbsp Chinese black vinegar

4 tsp Shaoxing wine

1 tsp sugar

1½ tsp light soy sauce

1 tsp crushed Sichuan peppercorns

12 sweet basil leaves

Red intestines with spinach
酥炸班指

This dish has a real kick from the spices in the cooking sauce. It requires two stages of cooking, but is well worth the effort. The flavour of yeast rice will take away some of the offal character of the intestines and its natural redness gives great contrast in the final dish.

To make the pig's intestines:

Wash the intestines thoroughly and turn inside out.

Mix all of the ingredients for the cooking sauce in a bowl. Taste and adjust for seasoning.

Bring a medium-sized pot of water to the boil and add the sauce and the intestines. You need enough water to cover the intestines.

Once the intestines are in the pot, turn down the heat to a gentle simmer and slow cook for an hour.

When the intestines are cooked, hang them up and allow them to cool and dry. The intestines can't be too dry as they will go black and if they are too wet, they won't crisp up.

⟶ *See over*

Makes 4 portions

1 length pig's intestines

For the red cooking sauce:

1 tbsp red fermented bean curd

1 tsp red rice yeast

1 cinnamon stick

2 star anise

2½ cm ginger, sliced

2 whole garlic cloves

1 spring onion, cut into three

5 slices of dried liquorice

To make the final dish:

Coat the intestines with cornflour inside and out and remove the excess.

Add a good glug of oil to a wok and heat until almost smoking. Deep-fry the intestines on a medium to high heat until crispy.

Meanwhile, blanch and refresh the spinach.

Mix all of the finishing sauce ingredients in a bowl and adjust the seasoning before heating through the sauce in a pan. Cook the sauce on a low heat.

When the intestine is crispy, place the spinach at the bottom of the plate in a hollow ring. Dollop the sauce into the middle and place the intestine on top. Garnish with ginger and serve.

For the final dish:

4 x 2½ cm lengths of cooked red intestine

cornflour to coat

10 spinach leaves

For the finishing sauce:

2½ tbsp tian mian jiang

5 tsp sweet chilli sauce

2½ tsp white wine vinegar

5 tsp Shaoxing wine

5 tbsp water

salt to taste

To garnish:

ginger to garnish

Tongue and ear salad
順風耳利

Cold offal is perfect for the summer. The pig's ear adds an unexpected texture and the sauce contains plenty of spice and acidity to keep this dish vibrant and interesting. The preserved vegetables offer a good crunch for a variety of textures within the dish.

To make the tongue and ear roll:

Cut the pig's ear in half from the hole of the ear. Char each half on a gas fire until the ear turns inside out. Scrape off any charred bits of the ear.

Cook the tongues briefly in boiling water until the surface of them changes colour – about 10 minutes. Remove the tongues from the heat and scrape off the white outer layers. They should peel away like skin.

Bring a medium-large pan of water to the boil – you need enough to cover the tongues and ear.

Add all of the ingredients for the stewing liquor to the water and adjust the seasoning.

Turn down the heat to a simmer and add the tongues and ear to the pan. Gently cook over a low heat in the simmering stewing liquor for an hour.

Remove the tongues and ear from the cooking liquor and allow to cool completely. Keep them separate as they will stick together. Reserve the cooking liquor.

Once cooled, place the tongues in the natural cup of the ears and wrap with string into a ballotine.

—› *See over*

Makes 6 portions

For the tongue and ear roll:

1 pig's ear

2 pig's tongues

cabage leaves

1 tbsp Shaoxing wine

1 tbsp Chinese black vinegar

30g palm sugar

2 tsp rose liqueur

2 tsp sesame

For the stewing liquor:

1 tbsp soy sauce

2 star anise

1 cinnamon stick

1 spring onion, cut into 3

1 tsp sugar

1 tsp Chinese five spice

1 tsp cumin

2 whole garlic cloves, skin on

Line the bottom of the pan with cabbage to stop the ballotines from sticking to the pan. Add the pig ear and tongue ballotines to the pan on top of the cabbage leaves and cover with the reserved cooking liquor. Add the Shaoxing wine, Chinese black vinegar and palm sugar to the pan. Turn the heat down even lower so only the occasional bubble will break the surface of the cooking liquor. Cook the ballotines for a further 30 minutes.

After cooking, allow the ballotine to cool in the cooking liquor.

When the ballotines are cool enough to touch, remove them from the cooking liquor and add a teaspoon each of rose liqueur and sesame oil. Wrap each ballotine in cling film

Allow the ballotines to cool completely before removing the cling film and cutting them into fine slices.

To make the final dish:

Mix all of the dressing ingredients in a bowl and adjust the seasoning to taste.

Place the pig's ears on top of the shredded lettuce and drizzle with the dressing.

Garnish with the preserved vegetables and sesame seeds before serving.

For the dressing:

6 tsp chilli sauce

6 tsp chilli oil

3 tsp sesame oil

3 tsp Chinese black vinegar

1½ tsp crushed Sichuan peppercorns

salt and sugar to taste

To serve:

finely chopped preserved vegetables

shredded lettuce

To garnish:

sesame seeds

Frog's legs with garlic chives
蒜苔燒田雞

Practice makes perfect with this dish. It's not the easiest dish to make but it's seriously impressive to pull off. It takes a lot of time, effort and practice so don't worry if you don't get it the first time. But when you get it right, it will taste amazing, and it looks spectacular too!

Cut each frog's leg in half, at the knee joint.

Scrape the meat off the bone of the smaller section. Lightly dust the meat with cornflour and set aside. On the other section of leg, scrape back the meat from the bones so that the meat is still attached to the bone at one end.

Lightly dust the inside of the leg meat with cornflour. Stuff the meat from the smaller section inside the hollowed inverse of the bigger section to create a convenient handle on your frog's leg.

Coat the entire frog's leg in a dusting of cornflour before dipping in a mix of three-parts egg to one-part water. Remove the excess liquid before deep-frying in a wok of hot oil till lightly golden.

Mix all the ingredients for the sauce together in a bowl and adjust the seasoning.

In a wok, heat through the sauce to thicken slightly before adding the frog's legs and cooking for 1 minute.

Just before the frog's legs are ready to come out, add the garlic chives to the pan and stir through until they just begin to wilt.

Serve with a garnish of spring onions.

Makes 6 portions

6 frog's legs

cornflour, to coat

1 egg, beaten

120g garlic chives, cut to 2½ cm lengths

2 tbsp water

For the sauce:

6 tbsp red chilli sauce

3 tsp white wine vinegar

2 tsp crushed Sichuan peppercorns

3 tsp tian mian jiang

6 tsp water

salt and sugar to taste

6 tsp slaked cornflour

To garnish:

chopped spring onions to garnish

Seafood
海鮮

Abalone with mushroom and pak choi
冬菇鮑魚

Abalone is probably not an ingredient you use every day. They can sometimes be a bit tricky to track down, but a good fishmonger or online retailer will be able to source them for you. Only the white stalk of the spring onion is used here because the stalk gives a clean and clear broth. Adding the green part of the spring onion will make the broth sticky. To make sure the abalones don't dry out, cook at least six at a time.

Remove the abalones from their shells and clean them thoroughly.

Heat all of the ingredients for the stewing liquor in a small pan. Bring to the boil and taste. Adjust seasoning if necessary.

Line the bottom of the pan with lettuce to prevent it from sticking and put the abalone on top. Cook the abalone slowly on a low temperature for 3 hours, covered with a lid. Add more stock if it begins to dry out.

When the abalones are cooked, remove them from the braising liquid, leave to cool, then slice finely.

Cook the shiitake mushrooms in a pan of hot water until they soften, about 10 minutes. Remove the stalk and cut it to the same thickness as the abalone.

Poach the pak choi in hot water until softened.

On a plate, put the pak choi at the bottom and place the sliced mushrooms on top. Arrange the sliced abalone on top of the mushroom.

Use the stewing liquor to make a sauce by heating it with the slaked cornflour until thickened. Add the white wine vinegar just before taking the sauce off the heat. Drizzle over the abalone and serve.

Makes 6 portions

6 abalones

6 pak choi leaves

6 dried shiitake mushrooms

6 tsp slaked cornflour

3 tsp white wine vinegar

For the stewing liquor:

12 slices of ginger

12 spring onion stalks

3 tbsp Shaoxing wine

6 tsp salt

3 tsp palm sugar

lettuce leaves

stock to cover

Crab noodle soup
酸菜蟹湯麵

Using a whole crab with its shell is essential to the flavour of this soup.
Thick noodles are best, as they really absorb the crab flavours.

Prepare the crab by removing the underbelly, the long, white dead man's fingers and the 'feet' (the pointy segments of the legs. Divide the crab into large pieces – cut the main body in half, separate the individual claws and allow two legs per portion. Rinse if required but be careful to retain the brown meat.

Dust all of the crab pieces generously with cornflour.

Heat plenty of oil in a wok, and deep-fry the crab until golden. This should take about 5-6 minutes. Remove and set aside.

In a separate wok, stir-fry the spring onions and ginger with the sesame oil. As they begin to take on colour, return the crab to the pan. Add the Shaoxing wine, salt, sugar, soy sauce and enough stock to cover the crab. The soup should be bubbling.

Cook for about a minute or so before adding the suan cai and the white wine vinegar. Cook for a further 5 minutes.

After 5 minutes, add the cooked noodles, shallot oil and the remaining tablespoon of sesame oil. Stir through before serving, ensuring the soup is piping hot.

Makes 6 portions

1 whole crab

cornflour, for dusting

oil, for frying

2 spring onions, cut into 2½ cm lengths

5 cm piece fresh ginger, sliced

1 tbsp sesame oil, plus 1 tbsp for serving

1 tbsp Shaoxing wine

1 tsp salt

½ tsp sugar

2 tsp light soy sauce

5 litres vegetable stock, for topping up the soup

1 suan cai leaf, finely chopped

1 tsp white wine vinegar

300g fresh cooked noodles

1 tsp shallot oil

Cuttlefish with lamb's kidney in *suan cai* sauce
紅白雙脆

Cuttlefish marries well with the kidney in this dish and *suan cai* brings great acidity. *Suan cai* is the same vegetable as *mei cai* used earlier in the book, but this version is preserved in brine rather than dried. Make sure you remove the network of veins inside the kidney otherwise when you cook it, the kidney will tighten and become chewy and inedible. Removing this network of sinews also takes away some of the kidney smells. Try squid, too, as an alternative to the cuttlefish.

Score the cuttlefish by cutting its surface with a knife but be careful not to cut completely through. In a small-medium pan, bring some water to a simmer and poach the cuttlefish for 2 minutes. Remove them from the water and set aside.

Warm a little oil to a wok, and stir-fry the suan cai with the spring onion, sweet basil, ginger and chilli. When the mixture becomes aromatic, add the sauce ingredients and stir through.

Once the sauce thickens, add the kidney and the cuttlefish and stir through.

Cook for a further minute before garnishing with deep-fried shallots. The kidneys should be slightly pink in the middle, but firm to the touch. Cook for a little longer if you prefer.

Makes 4 portions

4 bite-size portions cuttlefish

2 suan cai leaf, finely chopped

1 spring onion, finely chopped

12 sweet basil leaves

5 cm piece fresh ginger, minced

1 fresh red chilli, finely chopped

2 lamb's kidneys, cleaned and cut into bite-size slices

vegetable oil, for frying

For the sauce:

4 tbsp water

½ tsp sugar

1 tsp white wine vinegar

large pinch of ground white pepper

large pinch of salt

2 tsp slaked cornflour

To garnish:

deep-fried shallots

Octopus salad
涼拌八爪魚

May to September is the best time to eat octopus. As the flavours in the dressing are quite strong, something simple like shredded lettuce makes a good match. You can always use other vegetables as the base, just be sure to adjust the seasoning in the dressing accordingly. One octopus yields a lot of portions of this dish, which means you can't really scale down this recipe.

Put the whole octopus in a pan of cold salted water and bring to the boil. When the water begins to boil, bring down to a gentle simmer and cook the octopus for about 10 minutes.

After cooking, refresh immediately in cold water to stop the cooking process. Chill the octopus in the freezer.

Meanwhile, make the dressing by mixing together all of the ingredients in a bowl and adjust the seasoning.

When the octopus is completely cold and begins to set but is not frozen (roughly 30 minutes), remove from the freezer.

Cut the octopus into thin bite-size slices. You need about five slices per portion.

Serve the octopus on top of a bed of the vegetables and lettuce and drizzle over the dressing.

Garnish with a sprinkling of sesame seeds, chilli flakes and finely chopped spring onion to serve.

Makes 10 portions

1 octopus, about 150g, cleaned

For the dressing:

5 tbsp sweet chilli sauce

10 tsp Worcestershire sauce

5 tsp white wine vinegar

10 tsp prune sauce – mei zi jiang

1 tsp salt

5 spring onion stalks, finely chopped

5 tsp minced garlic

10 cm ginger

3 fresh red chillies, finely chopped

a few leaves of coriander or lettuce

10 tsp sesame oil

30 leaves sweet basil, finely chopped

To serve:

thinly sliced preserved (pickled) vegetables or shredded lettuce

To garnish:

sesame seeds, chilli flakes and finely chopped spring onion

Prawns with ginkgo nuts
白果蝦仁

Prawns and ginkgo nuts is a healthy combination and has a very delicate flavour. The ginkgo nuts in this dish are available in tins from Chinese shops and supermarkets. If you can't find ginkgo nuts, you can use tinned beans such as haricot or cannellini – just make sure they're cooked through first.

Poach the prawns and ginkgo nuts in a pan of hot water until the prawns have turned a pink colour, drain them and set aside.

Make the sauce by heating all of the ingredients together in a small pan on a gentle heat until thickened. Adjust the seasoning.

Once the sauce has thickened, add the prawns and ginkgo nuts. Add the shallot oil, and stir through before serving.

Makes 4 portions

8 fresh prawns, shelled and de-veined

50g ginkgo nuts, already cooked

1 tsp shallot oil

For the sauce:

1 fresh red chilli, roughly chopped

1 spring onion, roughly chopped

1 tbsp soy sauce

1 garlic clove, finely minced

1 tsp white wine vinegar

1 tsp sesame oil

1 tsp Shaoxing wine

1 tsp slaked cornflour

1 tbsp water

salt and sugar, to taste

Steamed prawn and spinach roll
鮮蝦鑲菠菜

This dish tastes so simple and delicious it can be a bit of surprise to find out it can be quite fiddly to make. The hardest part is butterflying the prawns but once you have mastered that, the rest is easy. Mince from chicken breast cooks more easily than mince from a different part of the chicken so you will need to adjust the cooking time if using the latter.

To butterfly the prawns and open them up, cut along the back of each prawn, de-veining as you go. Press down to flatten them.

Blanch the spinach in a pan of boiling water, then drain in a colander and refresh under cold running water. Squeeze out the excess water and finely chop the spinach.

Make the filling. In a bowl, mix the chicken mince with the water chestnuts, ½ tsp of salt, ½ tsp of sugar, the Shaoxing wine and the ground white pepper. Add the chopped spinach, then stir in a little of the cornflour to help the filling bind.

Bring a pan of water to a simmer and set your bamboo steamer on top.

Using a prawn as a wrapper, make a roll. To do this, put some of the filling on the feet end of the prawn and roll from the head to the tail. Press down gently to secure into a roll. Repeat with the rest of the prawns and the filling.

Coat the whole of each roll lightly with cornflour and put them on the plate you will be serving them on as you will be steaming them in the same dish,

Steam the rolls for about 5 minutes. When the prawns change colour, they are ready.

Meanwhile, make the sauce by heating the slaked cornflour

Makes 8 portions

8 large prawns, shelled

For the filling:

50g spinach

4 tsp chicken mince, from breast

4 tsp minced water chestnuts

½ tsp salt

½ tsp sugar

2 tsp Shaoxing wine

4 tsp ground white pepper

1 tsp cornflour, to coat and bind

For the sauce:

½ tsp slaked cornflour

100ml stock

1½ tsp egg white

salt, to taste

with the stock in a pan. As the mixture begins to thicken, add the egg white and stir through to disperse in the sauce. Season with salt to taste.

When the prawns are ready, spoon the sauce over them and drizzle the Shaoxing wine over the top. Garnish with shredded chilli and spring onion, and serve straight away.

To serve:

½ tsp Shaoxing wine

To garnish:

shredded red chilli and spring onion

Prawn toast with sweet and sour sauce
酸甜蝦卷

I've taken the prawn toast and flipped it on its side. Well, 'outside in' anyway. And spinach makes the perfect green accompaniment to this sweet and sour dish.

Trim the bread to remove the crusts.

Mix the minced prawns with a little salt in a bowl and place on one end of the bread. Roll up the bread, encasing the prawn mince, and seal the edges with the beaten egg.

Dip the ends of the roll in the egg before dipping in the sesame seeds. Set the rolls aside on a plate.

Meanwhile, blanch the spinach in a pan of boiling water, then drain in a colander and refresh under cold running water.

Heat a good glug of cooking oil in a wok until nearly smoking. Make sure that the oil is really hot before cooking the prawn toast, otherwise it can end up very oily.

Deep-fry the prawn toast in the hot oil for about 1 minute until golden. Once golden, carefully remove from the wok with a slotted spoon and allow to drain on kitchen paper before cutting in half diagonally.

Spoon the sweet and sour sauce on to a serving dish, put the prawn toast wedges on top, cut side up, and arrange the poached spinach between the two wedges. Sprinkle with sesame seeds and serve.

Makes 4 portions

4 slices thin-cut white bread

2 tbsp minced prawns
(see recipe for Steamed scallops with cucumber and prawns on page 192)

large pinch of salt

1 egg, beaten

2 tsp sesame seeds

2 tbsp shop-bought sweet and sour sauce

vegetable oil, for frying

30g spinach

To garnish:

sesame seeds

Prawn nests
龍鬚蝦球

Another name for this dish is 'dragon's whiskers' because the spirals are reminiscent of, well, dragon's whiskers. The best sauce for this is sweet and sour sauce, which makes it a great appetiser. Or, if you don't like sweet and sour sauce, a blend of salt and crushed Sichuan peppercorns is a good alternative.

Make the filling by mixing all the ingredients together in a bowl.

Roll the spring roll pastry into a tube and cut into slices so you end up with fine noodles of pastry about 5mm wide. Make sure the noodles are separated from each other.

Roll the prawn filling into balls about 2 cm in diameter. Press the pastry noodles around the filling to make a nest, encapsulating the filling. The nests are not meant to look neat.

Heat a good glug of oil in a wok until almost smoking.

Put the nests into the oil, one by one, making sure that they don't touch each other. Gently deep-fry on a medium heat until just golden. The nests burn easily, so be careful not to let this happen.

Meanwhile, warm the sweet and sour sauce in a pan with 2 teaspoons of water to serve with the prawn nests.

When the prawn nests are ready, serve on top of a spoonful of the warmed sweet and sour sauce and dress with shredded chilli.

Makes 4 portions

2 sheets spring roll pastry

For the filling:

12 minced prawns

1 water chestnut, minced

1 cm piece fresh ginger, minced

1 spring onion, thinly sliced

pinch of ground white pepper

1 tsp cornflour

salt, to taste

To serve:

4 tbsp sweet and sour sauce

To garnish:

shredded red chilli

Dry-fried prawns
椒鹽大蝦

Dry-fried prawns are highly addictive – these are hot, spicy, aromatic and crispy. The shell has all the flavour and adds a delicious crunch to this dish, so make sure you eat the prawns with the shells on!

De-vein the prawns and remove their heads and feet but keep the shells on.

Dust the prawns in cornflour. Dab on a little water to help the cornflour stick to the prawns if necessary.

Add a good glug of oil to a wok and heat until nearly smoking.

Deep-fry the prawns on a medium-high heat until they are golden.

Meanwhile, heat the Sichuan peppercorns, garlic and dried chillies in a separate pan with 1 tablespoon of oil and stir-fry for 1 minute until the mixture becomes fragrant.

When the prawns are ready, add them to the pan along with the spring onions and stir through. Add salt to taste and serve.

Makes 4 portions

8 large fresh prawns, in shells

cornflour, to coat

1 tsp Sichuan peppercorns

2 garlic cloves, thinly sliced

5 dried red chillies

2 spring onion stalks, cut into medallions

oil, for frying

salt, to taste

Scallops in spicy sauce
香蔥辣扇貝

The most important thing to remember with this dish is not to add the shallot oil until the end of cooking. Drizzle the shallot oil on just before serving as cooking with it will destroy the aromas. You can also garnish with spring onion but never use ginger and make sure you don't add the garnish to the scallops during cooking as this will change the flavours of the dish.

Make the sauce first by mixing all the ingredients together in a bowl. Taste and adjust the seasoning. Don't add too much salt as this will take away the flavour of the scallops.

The scallops are served in the dishes they are steamed, so make sure the dishes are heatproof and relatively sturdy. Place a scallop in the middle of each dish and dollop the spicy sauce on top.

Put the dishes in a bamboo steamer and steam for 5 minutes.

When the scallops are ready, drizzle the shallot oil on top. Sprinkle with sesame seeds and chopped coriander before serving.

Makes 4 portions

4 scallops, without shell or roe

2 tsp shallot oil

For the spicy sauce:

4 tsp Sichuan chilli sauce
(see recipe on page 252)

2 tsp tian mian jiang

1 tsp light soy sauce

2 tsp Shaoxing wine

2 tsp deep-fried shallot

1 tsp crushed Sichuan peppercorns

pinch of salt

To garnish:

sesame seeds

coriander

‛Drizzle the shallot oil on just before serving as cooking with it will destroy the aromas›

Scallop with asparagus and *dong cai* sauce
蘆筍冬菜扇貝

Dong cai is the preserved leaves of cabbages and is usually found in a jar or earthenware pot. It's salty and dry. The best *dong cai* comes from Tianjin in China, and is available at Chinese supermarkets or online. *Dong cai* is the key ingredient in this dish, as it gives the dish its unique flavour.

Bring a pan of water to a simmer and place a bamboo steamer on top.

For each portion, arrange the asparagus slices on the plate you will be serving this on and place the scallop on top. Steam the whole dish for 5 minutes.

Rinse the dong cai leaves to remove the excess salt and any sand, and finely chop.

To make the sauce, combine the garlic, stock, white pepper, and salt and sugar to taste in a small pan over a gentle heat. Add the dong cai and cook for 1 minute.

Add the slaked cornflour to the sauce and cook to thicken. Just before serving, add the white wine vinegar and sesame oil.

Remove the plate with the asparagus and scallop, drizzle the sauce on top, and serve.

Makes 4 portions

4 asparagus spears, thinly sliced

4 scallops

For the sauce:

4 dong cai leaves

4 cloves garlic, minced

200ml fish stock

pinch of ground white pepper

salt and sugar, to taste

3 tsp slaked cornflour

2 tsp white wine vinegar

2 tsp sesame oil

Steamed scallops
with cucumber and prawns
瓜鑲鮮貝

This scallop dish requires a little extra effort, but it tastes all the better for it. Make sure you use fresh scallops for this recipe as they not only taste better but are also generally much bigger than frozen scallops. The best way of making minced prawns is to smash the prawns with a knife as if you were smashing a clove of garlic. It gives a better texture.

First make the minced prawns by mixing all of the ingredients together in a bowl. You need only about 1 teaspoon of mince for each chunk of cucumber.

Bring a pan of water to a simmer and set your bamboo steamer on top.

Hollow out the cucumber pieces to form small cups. Blanch the cucumber briefly in a pan of boiling water. The cucumber should be just soft. Drain the cucumber in a colander and refresh under cold running water. Leave to cool completely.

Fill each cucumber cup with 1 teaspoon of minced prawns and place a scallop half on top, pressing it down gently. Make sure the cucumber is cold when you do this. Put the filled cucumber cups on the plate you will be serving them on as you will be steaming the scallops in the same dish.

Steam for around 5 minutes until the scallops are cooked through.

Meanwhile, make the sauce by heating the slaked cornflour with the stock until thickened. Check for seasoning. Just before you remove the sauce from the heat, add the egg white and stir through to disperse the egg. Then add the vinegar and sesame oil and remove from the heat.

When the scallops are ready, spoon the sauce over the top, followed by a drizzle of the chilli oil. Garnish with deep-fried shallots, and serve.

Makes 6 portions

3 scallops, without shell or roe, cut in half diagonally

6 x 2 cm discs of cucumber, peeled

For the minced prawns:

6 prawns, each no more than the length of your index finger

5mm piece fresh ginger, minced

1 cm spring onion stalk, very finely chopped

pinch of white pepper

½ tsp Shaoxing wine

pinch of sugar

pinch of salt

½ tsp cornflour

For the sauce:

1 tsp slaked cornflour

100ml fish stock

1½ tsp egg white

1½ tsp white wine vinegar

1½ tsp sesame oil

salt, to taste

To serve:

chilli oil

deep-fried shallots, to garnish

Stuffed baby squid
麻香鮮魷

Both chicken and prawn mince work well as a stuffing for the squid here, though chicken offers a greater contrast in texture after cooking. Try the squid with other sauces too, like sweet and sour sauce or sweet chilli sauce etc.

Blanch the baby squid in a pan of hot water briefly for about 1 minute, then transfer to a bowl of ice-cold water. The squid should shrink a little from the cooking.

To make the stuffing, mix all of the ingredients, except the chicken, together in a bowl. Adjust the seasoning if necessary, then mix in the chicken mince.

Drain the squid, then dust with cornflour and stuff each squid tube with the stuffing, taking care not to overfill them. The squid should only be slit open on one side.

Cover the opening, where the stuffing is exposed, with sesame seeds.

Heat a glug of oil in a wok until nearly smoking and shallow-fry the squid, sesame side down, on a high heat until golden. The oil should cover half of the squid. Be careful as this will splash a lot. Once the sesame seeds are golden, turn the squid over and cook the other side. It should take no more than 6 minutes altogether.

When the squid is ready, remove to a plate, dress with the Sichuan chilli sauce and serve.

Makes 4 portions

4 whole baby squid, cleaned and ready to use (ask your fishmonger to do this)

cornflour, to dust

sesame seeds, to coat

oil, for frying

For the stuffing:

10g coriander leaves, finely chopped

½ cm piece fresh ginger, minced

½ spring onion, minced

1 fresh red chilli, finely chopped

30g chicken mince

pinch of salt

To serve:

Sichuan chilli sauce
(see recipe on page 252)

Fish
魚肉

The Hunan fish

For banquets and bigger groups, a whole fish is often served. At Hunan, we have two ways of serving fish whole – with and without the bone. These methods work best for fish that don't have pin bones, like sea bass. For both methods though, the head and tail is reserved for presentation. You can always ask your fishmonger to do it for you but if you would like to try it yourself, here's how to prepare the fish for serving whole.

Without the bone – for flat presentation:

Gut and clean the fish by slitting open the fish from the stomach side.

Trim off any fins with scissors.

Cut along the gills up to the spine from the stomach opening on both sides of the fish to remove the head. You can trim and clean the head separately.

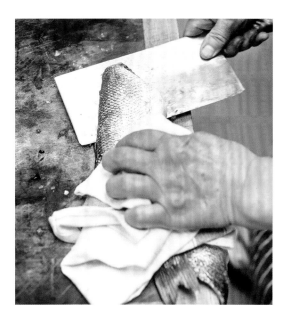

Lay the fish flat on a surface and cut along the spine to lift the fillet off the bones. Stop before you reach the tail. Repeat for the other fillet.

You will have two fillets separated from the spine but still joined at the tail.

Snip the spine near the tail end with scissors to remove it.

Flip the fillets over and remove any belly fat or bones that you missed.

Now you're left with two clean fillets attached to the tail and separated at the head, you're ready to cook.

To get the most out of the fillet, score the flesh side by cutting diagonally into the flesh but not through the skin.

With the bone – for round presentation:

Gut and clean the fish by slitting open the fish from the stomach side.

Trim off any fins with scissors.

To remove the fin along the backbone, trace the knife along both sides of the spine and then use scissors to cut the fin from the head and tail.

To score the fillet, cut the flesh diagonally all the way along the fish.

Rainbow monkfish
七彩鮟鱇

The name of this dish comes from how colourful it is. Anything so pleasing to look at will certainly be wonderful to eat!

Poach the monkfish in a pan of gently simmering salted water for about 3 minutes.

Add the mangetout, suan cai stalk and carrot and poach for 1 minute.

Meanwhile, combine all the sauce ingredients in a bowl, taste and adjust the seasoning.

After poaching the vegetables, drain the monkfish and vegetables, then return to the pan along with the spring onion, chilli and ginger. Add the sauce and warm through.

When the sauce has thickened, the dish is ready to serve.

Makes 4 portions

100g fillet of monkfish, cut into bite-sized pieces

4 mangetout, cut into 2½ cm slivers

1 suan cai leaf, stalk only, cut into 1 cm slivers

2½ cm piece carrot, cut into 1 cm slivers

1 spring onion, sliced diagonally into 1 cm slivers

½ fresh red chilli, cut into 1 cm slivers

2½ cm piece fresh ginger, cut into 1 cm slivers

For the sauce:

1 tbsp Shaoxing wine

1 tsp white wine vinegar

½ tsp ground white pepper

1 tsp sesame oil

1 tsp shallot oil

½ tsp slaked cornflour

1 tbsp water

salt and sugar, to taste

Fish roe with *Suan Cai*
酸菜漬魚卵

This recipe is made in two stages – the cod roe roll and the final dish.

Use any fish, chicken or prawn mince. The one we usually use is salmon.

To make the cod roe roll:

Steam the whole cod roe for around half an hour to cook through.

Mince the salmon using the side of your knife, as this gives the best texture.

Make the mince wrap by mixing all of the ingredients together. If you're unsure of the flavours, mix the seasonings together first in a bowl before adding to the mince and cornflour.

When the cod roe is done, allow to cool before cutting into eights, length-wise so you have eight portions of cod roe in the original length.

On a piece of cling film, spread the mince so it's the length of your cod roe. Put one of the eights of the cod roe on one end and roll up into a roll.

Freeze the rolls until firm with the cling film on before cutting into medallions.

To make the final dish:

Soak the wood ear mushroom in hot water until it softens.

Remove the cling film from your medallions and steam them on top of the wood ear mushroom for 10 minutes until they're cooked through.

Makes 8 portions

To make the cod roe roll:

1 length cod roe

For the wrap:

300g salmon

5 water chestnut, minced

1 cm ginger, minced

5 leaves of Vietnamese basil (jiu cheng ta), finely diced

2 tsp salt

1 tsp sugar

½ tbsp Shaoxing wine

1 tbsp cornflour

To make the final dish:

1 wood ear mushroom

red chilli to garnish

For the sauce:

½ leaf Chinese soured vegetable (suan cai), finely chopped

1 tsp Shaoxing wine

1 tsp soy sauce

2 tbsp stock

1 tsp slaked corn flour

black pepper

¼ tsp white wine vinegar

salt and sugar to taste

Sea bass with tofu roll
紫菜豆腐蒸魚

Sea bass and tofu may sound like an unusual combination but it gives a great contrast in texture. The flexibility of this dish means that it works with any sort of tofu and any sort of fish. Whatever the ingredients though, you need to make sure it's in bite-size portions so you can eat it in one go.

Make the sauce by mixing together all of the sauce ingredients together in a bowl. Adjust the seasoning.

On a flat surface, roll the tofu in the nori, following its shape, to form a tube. If the nori is too dry, dampen it slightly. With a very sharp knife, cut the roll into 2 cm lengths and put each portion on a separate plate.

Divide the sea bass fillet equally according to the number of cut rolls you have. Each portion of fish should be around 2 cm by 3 cm in size.

Put some water in a pan to simmer, and set your bamboo steamer on the top.

Drape the portions of sea bass over the top of the rolls, drizzle the sauce on top and steam for about five minutes until the rolls are cooked through.

When the rolls are ready, drizzle with the shallot oil, garnish with red chillies and deep-fried shallots and serve.

Makes 6 portions

1 tube of silken tofu
(should be packs of around 250g)

1 sheet nori seaweed

1 fillet of sea bass

For the sauce:

2 spring onions, finely chopped

4 tsp light soy sauce

4 tsp Shaoxing wine

2 tsp malt vinegar

2½ cm ginger, finely sliced

salt and sugar to taste

To garnish:

1 tsp shallot oil per portion

red chillies and fried shallots

Steamed sea bass with ginger and spring onion
薑蔥蒸魚

You have to use very fresh fish for this dish as it's this freshness that the sauce is bringing to life. And eat as soon as it's ready; when it's cold, the freshness will disappear.

Prepare the fish by removing all the bones according to the instructions at the beginning of this section (page 206) to keep the fillets intact with the tail. The fillets should sit flat with the skin side down.

Place a large bamboo steamer over a pan of simmering water. On a big plate, steam the fish with the ginger and spring onion for about twenty minutes until cooked.

Meanwhile, make the sauce by mixing all of the ingredients in a bowl. Taste and adjust the seasoning before heating the sauce in a very small pan.

When the fish is cooked, drizzle the sauce over the top and serve.

Makes 6 portions

1 sea bass

1 cm ginger, finely sliced

½ spring onion, finely chopped

Sauce:

1 tsp light soy sauce

½ tsp sesame oil

½ spring onion, finely chopped

1 cm ginger, finely sliced

Deep-fried sea bass with chilli sauce

豆瓣溜鱸魚

In Chinese food culture, nose-to-tail eating is nothing new. Fish, in dishes like this, are always served whole, heads and all, because it signifies start to finish. Of course at home you don't have to serve the head. The flavours in the sauce are very strong so there's no need to marinate the fish beforehand or add additional seasoning to the cornflour. Make sure you don't ladle the sauce over the fish until you're ready to serve, so that the fish will still be crispy at the table.

Prepare the fish so that the fillets remain attached to the tail (see instructions on pages 204-209).

Slice the fillets in half diagonally, without slicing through the skin, to achieve a gilled effect with the flesh.

Heat a good glug of oil in a wok until nearly smoking.

Dampen the fish slightly before dusting with cornflour. To keep the tail standing up during cooking, pull it under and over between the two fillets with the fish facing skin side down. Now hold on to the tail as you put the fish into the hot oil (it's advisable to wear oven gloves) and make sure the fillets are fixed in position before dropping the tail in the oil.

Deep-fry on a high heat until the outside of the fish is golden. This will take around 10 minutes depending on the size of your fish.

Meanwhile, mix all the sauce ingredients, apart from the slaked cornflour, in a bowl. Taste and adjust the seasoning if necessary. In a small pan, heat the sauce ingredients on a low heat to bring out their aromas.

When the sauce is warm, stir in the slaked cornflour and heat gently to thicken. The sauce is ready once it has thickened.

When the fish is cooked, remove it to a serving plate, then ladle the sauce over the top and serve garnished with chopped spring onion.

Makes 6 portions

1 whole sea bass

cornflour, to coat

oil, for deep-frying

For the sauce:

1 tbsp spicy douban paste or fermented black bean sauce

2 tsp red chilli sauce (see recipe on page 250)

2 cloves garlic, minced

1 cm piece fresh ginger, finely chopped

2 water chestnuts, smashed

1 tsp Shaoxing wine

2 tbsp water

1 tsp white wine vinegar

2 tsp vegetable oil

1 tsp sugar

1 tsp slaked cornflour

To garnish:

chopped spring onion

Steamed salmon, cod and chicken parcels
燴蒸雙鮮

You can use any delicate fish instead of cod in this recipe. White fish such as haddock or hake works particularly well but oily fish such as mackerel would overwhelm the salmon. Mince the fish with a knife to achieve the right consistency and texture. You can also substitute the chicken with prawns .

Mix all of the ingredients for the filling together in a bowl.

Form the filling mixture into about 16 balls about 2 cm in diameter.

Cut the salmon into about 16 very thin square slices.

Place each cod and chicken ball on a slice of salmon and fold in the ends of the salmon to form parcels.

Place the parcels into the bowls that you're going to serve them in. You should have a portion in each bowl.

Bring a pan of water to a gentle simmer and set your bamboo steamer on top.

Steam the parcels for 10 minutes in the bowl until the filling is cooked through.

Meanwhile, make the dressing by heating the stock, cornflour, and salt and sugar to taste in a pan until it begins to thicken. Add the egg white and mix thoroughly so that it is dispersed throughout the dressing. Add the vinegar and sesame oil and stir through just before serving.

When the parcels are cooked, remove from the steamer, pour the dressing over them and drizzle with a little chilli oil.

Makes 8 portions

1 skinless salmon fillet

For the filling:

5g coriander stalks, finely chopped

½ spring onion, finely chopped

½ cm piece fresh ginger, finely chopped

½ tsp salt

½ tsp sugar

½ tbsp cornflour

small pinch white pepper

1½ tbsp deep-fried shallots

¼ cod fillet, minced

½ chicken breast, minced

3 water chestnuts, minced

For the dressing:

50ml chicken stock

½ tsp slaked cornflour

salt and sugar, to taste

½ egg white

¼ tsp white wine vinegar

¼ tsp sesame oil

To serve:

chilli oil

Skate wings with spinach and baby olives
清蒸破布子魚鰭佐菠菜

This is a dish of simple flavours. The skate wing is a delicate fish and the baby olives really help to add savoury notes to the dish. But the Chinese sausage for the garnish is probably the most important element – it makes the whole dish come to life with delicious aromas.

Cut the skate wing into 6 roughly equal portions.

Bring a pot of stock to the boil before adding the skate wings and turning down the heat to a gentle simmer. Poach the wings in the stock for about 5 minutes until the fish is cooked. Reserve the stock.

Meanwhile, blanch and refresh the spinach.

Once the skate wing is done, remove and set aside. Keep it warm with the spinach.

Make a sauce by heating the baby olives in 3 tbsp of the stock. Add the slaked cornflour to thicken and adjust seasoning.

Arrange the portions of skate wing around the serving plate with the spinach in the middle.

Drizzle the sauce over the top along with a little chilli oil, a sprinkling of the Chinese sausage, the red chillies and serve.

Makes 6 portions

1 skate wing

5 leaves of spinach

1tbsp baby olives

1tsp slaked corn flour

1tsp chilli oil

stock, enough to cover

salt to taste

To garnish:

finely chopped Chinese sausage
fresh red chillies

‘ Baby olives really help to add
savoury notes to the dish ’

Salmon and prawn rolls on wood ear mushrooms

雲耳蒸鮮

Use fresh salmon for the wrap as frozen fish will disintegrate during cooking. The earthy wood ear mushrooms at the base complement the freshness of the seafood but you can also use a milder accompaniment such as tofu or greens.

In a bowl or jug, soften the wood ear mushrooms in a little hot water. This should take about 20 minutes.

In a separate bowl, mix the minced prawns with the minced ginger.

Cut the salmon lengthways into thin slices about 3 mm thick, so that they can be used as wraps.

Spoon the minced prawn mixture into the middle of each slice and roll into tubes.

Plug the ends of the tubes with the minced water chestnuts.

Bring a pan of water to a simmer, and set your bamboo steamer on top.

Drain the mushrooms and transfer to 2 small heatproof plates. Place the stuffed salmon tubes on top of the mushrooms and drizzle the Shaoxing wine over them.

Steam for around 5 minutes until the fish is cooked.

Meanwhile, make the dressing by heating all the ingredients together in a small pan.

When the salmon and prawn rolls are ready, drizzle with the dressing and garnish with sliced red chillies and spring onions before serving.

Makes 4 portions

40g wood ear mushrooms

2 x 50g salmon fillet, about 6 cm square

250g minced prawns (see recipe for Steamed scallops with cucumber and prawns on page 192)

1 cm piece fresh ginger, minced

6 water chestnuts, minced

¼ tsp Shaoxing wine

For the dressing:

60ml chicken stock

1 tsp slaked cornflour

½ tsp white wine vinegar

½ tsp light soy sauce

½ tsp sesame oil

salt to taste

To garnish:

sliced fresh red chillies and spring onions

Vegetables
菜

Chilli stir-fried cabbage
宮保高麗菜

For this dish the wok must be really hot in order to cook the vegetables quickly so they maintain a slight crunch. Sprinkle the oil with salt before adding the cabbage and make sure the cabbage is dry before putting it into the pan. You can use any type of cabbage you want, but make sure you adjust the cooking time and amount of stock accordingly.

Add a glug of oil to a hot wok and heat until it's just beginning to smoke.

Add a pinch of salt to the wok, then add the cabbage, chillies and Sichuan peppercorns.

Stir-fry for about 2 minutes before adding the chilli oil, stock, sugar and salt to taste.

Continue to stir-fry until most of the stock has evaporated, then stir through the white wine vinegar. Adjust for seasoning before serving.

Makes 6 portions

½ head of cabbage, roughly chopped

3 dried red chillies, broken in two

1 tsp crushed Sichuan peppercorns

1½ tsp red chilli oil

1 tbsp stock

¼ tsp white wine vinegar

salt and sugar to taste

French chips
椒鹽四季豆

This dish is a real classic at Hunan. It's called French chips because it's made with French beans but everyone thinks it tastes like chips. Our secret? We use self-raising flour for the batter.

Make the batter first by mixing the flour with the water, vinegar and salt in a bowl. You need quite a thick and gloopy batter that will generously coat the French beans. Adjust the amount of water if necessary.

Let the batter rest until it begins to bubble before using. This should take around 20 minutes.

Heat a good glug of oil in a wok until it's almost smoking.

Coat the French beans with the batter, let any excess run off and carefully put them, one by one, into the hot oil, making sure that they don't touch each other.

Deep-fry the French beans until they start to turn golden. This will take about 1 minute. Carefully remove from the oil with a slotted spoon and drain on kitchen paper.

In a dry wok, stir-fry the chilli with the spring onion and garlic on a medium heat until they become aromatic. Add the French beans and stir through the seasoning before serving.

Makes 6 portions

100g French beans, trimmed

oil, for deep-frying

For the batter:

50g self-raising flour

100ml water

2 tsp white wine vinegar

small pinch of salt

To stir-fry:

1 fresh red chilli, finely sliced

1 garlic clove, minced

½ spring onion, finely sliced

salt and crushed Sichuan peppercorns, to taste

Pumpkin balls
金瓜香球

These pumpkin balls are delicious as a snack and are perfect during the autumn months when pumpkin is in season. Idcally you need one leaf of lettuce per pumpkin ball to serve. The natural curve of the leaves helps to capture the sauce so you can eat it all together.

Peel the pumpkin and remove the seeds and discard. Cut the pumpkin into small chunks and steam in a bamboo steamer set over a pan of simmering water for 15 minutes until it softens.

When the pumpkin softens, remove to a bowl and mix into a rough mash.

Add the pumpkin seeds, flour and salt to the steamed pumpkin chunks and mix together quickly. If the mixture is too mushy, chill it in the fridge until firmer.

Form the pumpkin mixture into 12 balls, about the size of a golf ball, and stud all over with the cubed bread.

Mix all of the ingredients for the dressing together in a bowl and adjust the seasoning.

Heat a generous amount of oil in a wok until almost smoking.

Deep-fry the pumpkin balls on a medium heat until golden. Remove with a slotted spoon and set aside on kitchen paper to drain.

Place 2 pumpkin balls on top of a lettuce leaf and drizzle with a little of the dressing to serve.

Makes 6 portions

500g pumpkin
(about ½ medium-sized pumpkin)

1 tbsp shelled pumpkin seeds

1 tbsp plain flour

1/3 tsp salt

4 thick slices white bread, crusts removed, cubed to 5 mm cubes

For the dressing:

2 tbsp golden syrup

2 tbsp sweet chilli sauce

1 tbsp water

1 cm piece fresh ginger, finely chopped

1 spring onion, roughly chopped

2 tsp sesame oil

2 tsp chilli oil

1 tsp white wine vinegar

To serve:

lettuce

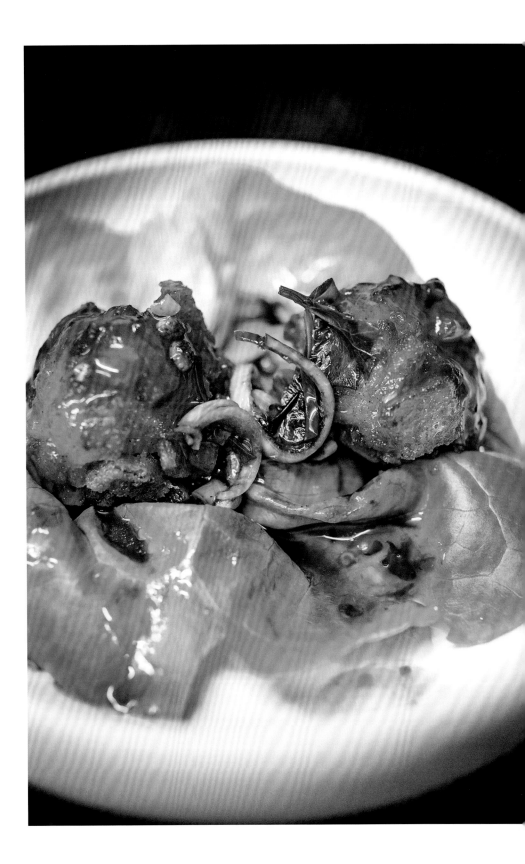

Crispy tofu sticks
蘇梅竹枝

Tofu sticks are already dry and when you deep-fry them, they become very aromatic. A light coating of dressing means that thc tofu sticks will acquire the much-needed acidity to make them even more delicious.

Heat a large amount of oil in a wok and deep-fry the tofu sticks until crispy. Once crispy, take them out of the wok and leave them to drain on some kitchen paper.

Mix the dressing in a bowl and season to taste.

Toss the fried tofu sticks through the dressing for a light coating.

Serve on top of shredded lettuce and garnish with coriander leaf.

Makes 4 portions

100g dried tofu stick

For the dressing:

2 tbsp sweet chilli sauce

1 tbsp plum sauce

2 tsp white wine vinegar

2 tsp sesame oil

2 tsp honey

2 cm ginger, minced

½ tsp minced garlic

salt to taste

To serve:

shredded lettuce

To garnish:
coriander and sesame seeds

Tofu and bean sprout salad
涼拌銀芽豆腐

This salad may seem simple, but the sauce really elevates it to more than the sum of its parts. Sesame paste really highlights the mellow aromas in the deep-fried tofu while the vinegar and chilli sauce really add a kick to the flavour. If you're looking for extra crunch, sprinkle some chopped cashew nuts on top.

Heat a good glug of oil in a wok until nearly smoking. Deep-fry the tofu strips in the oil for about 2 minutes, until golden and crispy.

Blanch the bean sprouts in a pan of boiling water briefly, then drain in a colander and refresh under cold running water – you want them to still have a slight crunch.

Meanwhile, mix the ingredients for the sauce together in a bowl. Taste and adjust the seasoning if necessary.

Mix the tofu and bean sprouts together in a serving dish and dress with the sauce.

Garnish with spring onion and ginger, and serve.

Makes 4 portions

100g tofu, cut into strips

50g bean sprouts

oil, for deep-frying

For the sauce:

½ tbsp sesame paste or tahini

1 cm piece fresh ginger, minced

1 garlic clove, minced

1 tsp soy sauce

1 tsp white wine vinegar

1 tsp red chilli sauce
(see recipe on page 250)

salt and sugar, to taste

½ tsp crushed Sichuan peppercorns

To garnish:

spring onion, finely chopped

fresh ginger, finely chopped

Tofu spinach roll
腐皮菠菜卷

Here's a recipe that's been on the Hunan menu since we opened the restaurant. It's a bit tricky to make but it's worth it for the contrast of the tender spinach on the inside and the crispy tofu shell on the outside.

Blanch the spinach in a pan of boiling water, then drain well in a colander and refresh under cold running water. Using your hands, squeeze out as much water from the spinach leaves as possible.

Blanch the mushrooms in boiling water and refresh as above. Do the same with the water chestnuts and then the bamboo shoots.

Make the filling. In a bowl, mix the spinach with the mushrooms, water chestnuts, bamboo shoots, salt, ground white pepper and sesame oil.

For the tofu roll, mix the self-raising flour and water in a separate bowl to make a runny paste. It needs to be easily spreadable on the tofu skin.

Place the tofu skin in front of you with one corner pointing towards you.

Place the spinach filling about a third of the way up from the corner near to you, and 2½ cm in from each side.

Bring up the tofu skin to cover the filling and roll up until you're halfway up the tofu skin, level with the two corners on either side.

Apply the paste to the edges of the remaining tofu skin, then fold in both corners and roll up.

Mix the 2 teaspoons of cornflour with the leftover paste to thicken it. It should be quite viscous at this stage.

Heat a generous amount of oil in a wok until it's almost smoking.

Coat the entire spinach roll with a thin layer of the paste and deep-fry on a high heat until it sets. Remove from the oil with a slotted spoon and drain on kitchen paper. Leave to cool.

Makes 6 portions

For the filling:

500g spinach

2 dried Chinese mushrooms, reconstituted and thinly sliced

2 water chestnuts, thinly sliced

50g shredded bamboo shoots

pinch of salt

½ tsp ground white pepper

½ tsp sesame oil

For the tofu roll:

3 tbsp self-raising flour

5 tbsp water

1 piece tofu skin, about 30cm square

2 tsp cornflour

oil, for deep-frying

sesame seeds, to coat

Turn off the heat but keep the pan on the hob as you'll be using it again later.

Once cooled, cut the roll into 2½ cm sections. Tip some sesame seeds into a bowl.

Taking one spinach parcel at a time, dip the cut ends into the remaining flour paste and then into the sesame seeds to coat them, then set aside. Make up more flour paste if necessary.

To make the sauce, heat a little oil in a heavy-bottomed pan and stir-fry the spring onion and minced garlic together until fragrant.

To a bowl, add the rest of the sauce ingredients, apart from the cornflour and the sesame oil, mix well and adjust the seasoning. Once you're happy with the flavours, add the cornflour and sesame oil.

Add the sauce to the spring onion and garlic and heat through until the sauce thickens.

Meanwhile, reheat the oil in the wok, then carefully add the spinach parcels and deep-fry on a high heat once more until golden.

Once the spinach parcels are ready, remove to kitchen paper to drain. Transfer to serving plates, then drizzle the sauce over the top and serve.

For the sauce:

½ spring onion, finely chopped

1 clove garlic, minced

1½ tbsp water

¼ tsp chilli powder

¼ fresh red chilli, finely chopped

1 tsp tomato ketchup

pinch of salt

¼ tsp cornflour

½ tsp sesame oil

Mustard greens and tofu
雪裡紅豆腐干

Mustard greens can be quite intense and that's why you need the other vegetables to balance them out. The mix of vegetables will also bring a great variety of textures to the plate.

On a high heat, stir-fry the minced garlic and spring onion briefly in a wok until they become aromatic.

Add the mustard greens and stir through until they just begin to wilt.

Add the rest of the vegetables and the tofu and stir through with salt and sugar for a further minute.

Add the Shaoxing wine, white wine vinegar and chilli just before serving.

Makes 4 portions

1 tsp minced garlic

1 spring onion stalk, roughly chopped

3 leaves mustard greens, roughly chopped

2 slices lotus root, roughly chopped

1 piece five spice tofu, cubed

2½ cm carrot, cubed

1 dried Chinese mushroom, reconstituted and roughly chopped

¼ tsp salt

¼ tsp sugar

1 tsp Shaoxing wine

½ tsp white wine vinegar

1 chilli, finely sliced

The intensity of the mustard greens can be quite unforgiving and that's why you need the other vegetables to balance it out

Sauces
醬料

Red chilli sauce
紅辣椒醬

Slow cooking is the only way to extract the full flavours from the chillies in this spicy sauce. The chilli powder is very dry and will soak up most of the liquid so take care to ensure it doesn't burn. We use this in a variety of dishes such as red oil beef, and it has a more mellow rounded spice than the Sichuan chilli sauce.

In a bowl, mix the water, stock, tomato purée, tian mian jiang, chilli flakes, chilli powder, salt and sugar together and adjust for seasoning.

Heat the mixture in a wok with 2 tablespoons of oil until it becomes fragrant.

Add the remaining tablespoon of oil and stir through.

Dilute with more stock if necessary. You need a thick but runny sauce with the consistency of salad cream.

Makes about 300ml

5 tbsp water

5 tbsp chicken stock

1 tbsp tomato purée

2 tsp tian mian jiang

1 tbsp chilli powder

3 tbsp chilli flakes

½ tsp salt

½ tsp granulated sugar

2 tbsp oil, plus 1 tbsp

Sichuan chilli sauce
椒麻辣醬

This punchy sauce is essential to Hunan's cooking, and the Sichuan peppercorns lend their characteristic numbing spice to many of our dishes. You need a lot of oil to make this sauce as it captures the flavours of the chilli and also helps to preserve it. When the sauce settles, you should have a layer of oil on top. If you add too much, you can always use the excess as chilli oil. This sauce is much spicier than the red chilli sauce.

Add the chilli flakes to a hot wok with about a tablespoon of cooking oil. Heat the chilli flakes until the pan begins to smoke, stirring constantly to avoid burning. Be careful as it will spit a little and there will be a lot of smoke.

As the chilli flakes absorb the cooking oil, add more oil one tablespoon at a time until you have a paste. It should take around five minutes.

When the chilli flakes begin to darken, add the Sichuan peppercorns off the heat with 3 tbsp of stock. Stir through and return to the hob on a medium heat.

Add the tian mian jiang, tomato purée and the remaining stock with salt and sugar.

Stir through all the ingredients, adding more stock and oil if necessary. You need a thick but runny sauce.

Finally add the white wine vinegar and stir through just before taking it off the heat.

Makes about 300ml

2 tbsp crushed Sichuan peppercorns

4 tbsp chilli flakes

2 tsp tian mian jiang

2 tsp tomato purée

200ml cooking oil

1 tsp white wine vinegar

6 tbsp chicken stock plus more if necessary

Acknowledgements

This cookbook has been a long time in the making; not just over the months it took to write but also during the many years in which it has been a project on the horizon.

So it's really with the sincerest gratitude that I'd like to thank the following people:

First and foremost my thanks goes to my family and friends for their support over the years. Without them I wouldn't have been able to achieve the things that I have.

The staff at Hunan, for their ceaseless hard work. That has been integral to the restaurant's success.

Our wonderful suppliers who keep us stocked with fantastic ingredients. Especially Andy, Matthew and Mel at Southbank Fish; Darragh and Michael at O'Shea's; and Ronnie, James and Albert from Cook's Delight.

Dino Joannides, my friend and a long-time supporter of Hunan, for making the introductions that finally got this project going.

Trevor Dolby and Katherine Murphy, for their hard work at Random House in giving me an opportunity to make my vision a reality.

Paul Winch-Furness, who has been meticulously capturing just the right moments so that we could have so many stunning images for the book.

Keira Yang and Felix von Bomhard at By Associates, for their creativity and flair in making the book so beautiful.

And last but not least, Qin Xie, for her patience in the kitchen and at the table, scribbling down all my thoughts and putting the words on to the pages.

Index of recipes

Index of ingredients

store cupboard 28

sugar 34

sweet and sour sauce, prawn toast with 182, 183

temperature 26

Tian mian jiang 35

TOFU:

crispy tofu sticks 238, 239

mustard greens and tofu 246, 247

sea bass with tofu roll 214, 215

tofu and bean sprout salad 240, 241

tofu spinach roll 244, 245

tripe in spicy sauce 148, 149

trotters, stuffed pig's with pak choi 114, 115, 116, 117

vegetables 230–47 *see also under individual type of vegetable*

vinegar 27, 37

Chinese black vinegar 37

red wine vinegar 37

white wine vinegar 37

water chestnut parcels, chicken and 66, 67

white beans, prawns with 178, 179

white wine vinegar 37

WINE:

Shaoxing wine 32

wok, the 27

Qin Xie is a food, drink and travel journalist reporting frequently on chefs, restaurants, wines and destinations. She has written widely for publications including CNN, Yahoo, *Financial Times* and *The Times*. Her reportage has covered everything from Georgian Qvevri wines and Belgian elixirs to cacao from the Dominican Republic and Basmati rice from India.

Whilst working as a journalist, she also received classical culinary training at Leith's School of Food and Wine and subsequently completed kitchen and pastry stages at Michelin-starred restaurants including The Fat Duck, Dinner by Heston Blumenthal, The Square and Lima.

Born in the UNESCO City of Gastronomy, Chengdu, she has a deep-rooted understanding and appreciation of Chinese food and is in constant pursuit of authenticity – something she found at Hunan.

She keeps a blog of her gastro-adventures at In Pursuit of Food (inpursuitoffood.com).

Paul Winch-Furness is a professional food and restaurant photographer. He has many years of experience shooting in studios and on location and his work has featured in a variety of magazines and newspapers. He is regularly commissioned by the newest London restaurants to shoot their food, interiors and staff for use in various media and publicity.

He has embraced social media including Instagram, Facebook and Twitter as a means of communicating directly with his audience and this has given work an added dimension since he is often asked to Instagram his meal by the restaurants he frequents.

Paul has a BA in photography from then University of Westminster and an MA in Photography from LCC and has taught at both Westminster University and runs his own photography workshops.

Published by Preface 2014

10 9 8 7 6 5 4

Copyright © Mr Y. S. Peng & Qin Xie 2014

Mr Y. S. Peng & Qin Xie have asserted their right to be identified as the authors
of this work under the Copyright, Designs and Patents Act 1988

First published in Great Britain in 2014 by Preface Publishing

20 Vauxhall Bridge Road
London, SW1V 2SA

An imprint of The Random House Group Limited

www.penguin.co.uk

Addresses for companies within The Random House Group Limited
can be found at www.randomhouse.co.uk

The Random House Group Limited Reg. No. 954009

A CIP catalogue record for this book is available from the British Library

ISBN 978 1 848 09434 5

www.greenpenguin.co.uk

Penguin Random House is committed to a sustainable future for
our business, our readers and our planet. This book is made from
Forest Stewardship Council® certified paper.

Typeset and designed by By Associates

Photographs © Paul Winch-Furness

Printed and bound in China by C&C Offset Printing Co., Ltd.